COLUMBA'S ISLAND

COLUMBA'S ISLAND

Iona from Past to Present

E. MAIRI MACARTHUR

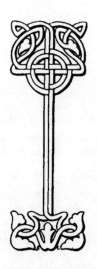

EDINBURGH UNIVERSITY PRESS

Dedicated to my aunt,
Mary MacArthur,
with thanks for many happy holidays

© E. Mairi MacArthur, 1995

Edinburgh University Press Ltd
22 George Square, Edinburgh

Reprinted 1996

Typeset in Linotron Caledonia
by Nene Phototypesetters Ltd, Northampton,
and printed and bound in Great Britain
by BPC Wheatons Ltd, Exeter

A CIP record for this book is available
from the British Library

ISBN 0 7486 0737 4

The publisher wishes to acknowledge subsidy from the
Scottish Arts Council towards the publication of this book.

Contents

Acknowledgements

I acknowledge with thanks receipt of a travel and research grant from the Scottish Arts Council towards the costs of researching this book. I am most grateful to the following individuals and institutions for permission to consult archives or papers and for assistance during the research: His Grace the Duke of Argyll and Alastair Campbell of Airds, Inveraray Castle; Murdo MacDonald, Argyll and Bute District Council Archives; John Barber and Jerry O'Sullivan, AOC Scotland; Crichton Lang and Lawrence Marshall, Iona Cathedral Trust; the *Oban Times*; Robert Smart, University Muniments, University of St Andrews; the Russell Trust; Ian Fisher, the Royal Commission on the Ancient and Historical Monuments of Scotland; and Dr Margaret Mackay, School of Scottish Studies. The Celtic designs are reproduced, with permission, from *The Celtic Art of Iona* by Iain MacCormick. I am also indebted, for much advice and support cheerfully given, to my colleague Dr Simon Taylor.

E. Mairi MacArthur

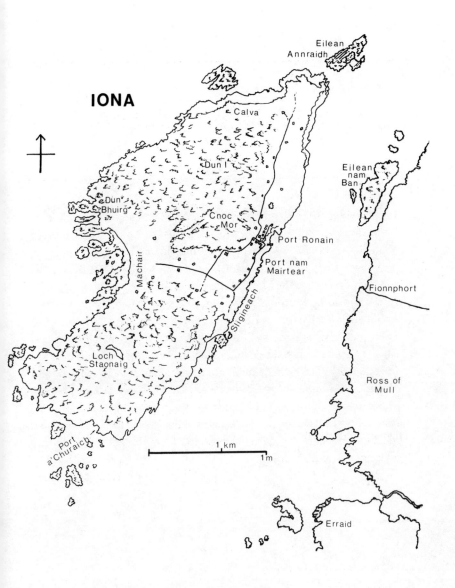

Frontispiece Crofters' harvest at Clachanach and, in the foreground left, behind Bishop's Walk. In the middle distance can be seen the west portion of the vallum, enclosing the former monastic site. Photographed by Donald B. MacCulloch in 1938, the Iona Community's first living quarters, a wooden hut, is to the left of the cathedral.

Preface

'There will soon be quite a library of books about Iona ...' wrote a young man called Henry Davenport Graham to his father in August 1849. A guest in the Free Church manse, he had made some very fine drawings of the island's carved stones which were shortly to be published, at the request of the Duke of Argyll, under the title *Antiquities of Iona*.

A couple of guidebooks were already in print, as was an American clergyman's travelogue and a tract by an Anglican bishop. Graham had just met two Frenchmen sketching on the island for a forthcoming publication and went on: 'So poor Iona is going to be dragged before the public now, Scotchmen, Englishmen and Frenchmen, High Church, Low Church and no church, Bishops, Dukes and commoners have all set upon it tooth and nail!'

Just what Graham would have made of the vast volume of literature available about Iona today defies the imagination. Yet his own work was one of the first to highlight an important strand in the island's history, its artistic legacy, one of the aspects that have inspired so much fascination over so many centuries. It is always legitimate, however, to ask the question: why write another book about Iona?

The answer lies in the awareness that there are basically two Iona stories. One is very well known and has been documented by many. The other is overshadowed to some degree by the first and seldom 'dragged before the public' in print. A few years ago I was lucky enough to have the opportunity to study this less familiar history, that of the local population, at the School of Scottish Studies in Edinburgh. The resulting thesis was published by Edinburgh University Press in 1990 as a book, *Iona: The Living Memory of a Crofting Community 1750-1914*.

The huge amount of material collected in the course of that research, from a range of documentary and oral sources, led to the idea of taking the social history of the islanders a little further forward – through two world wars, through the changes of the twentieth century, and through events of wider significance such as the creation of the Iona Cathedral Trust and the arrival in their midst of the Iona Community. Little had been written about this, still less from a local point of view. In 1979 a car-ferry service began across the Sound of Iona and the locals were effectively linked up, under their own steam if they so chose, to anywhere on the mainland. That same year the island was sold, after having been in the ownership of the Dukes of Argyll for nearly three centuries. This seemed an appropriate point to close the chronological narrative, although I have added a postscript of my own.

But what of that first and famous story of Iona, of monks and missionaries and ministers? It seemed worthwhile to take a fresh look at St Columba, and at what came after him down the ages. There are always new questions to pose, alternative interpretations to explore. In particular I wanted to keep in mind two simple facts: that people have lived on the island from before Columban times until today, and that they have been supported throughout, in part at least, by the same resources of land and sea.

This is not a standard academic study, if such a thing exists. I have no background in any of the disciplines – such as economic history, historical geography or social anthropology – on which the examination of a particular community is often based. Rather, it is a portrait of a place and its people using, as one set of primary sources, what can be read from the landscape and what has been passed down through oral tradition. This type of information can rarely tell the whole story in isolation, but what it frequently can do is amplify or complement the written record contained in estate archives, official papers and books. And it can breathe life into the tale.

This book contains a lot of names, of real people and real places. It is at times highly personal and anecdotal, and makes no claim always to be totally objective, as I am too close to the subject for that. To steal Dr Johnson's sentiments, expressed when he landed on Iona: 'To abstract the mind from all emotion would be impossible, if it were endeavoured, and foolish if it were possible'. The narrative touches on national events but also describes the minutiae of the daily round. Snapshots of certain aspects or periods have been selected, for it would be impossible to cover everything. Events at Clachanach, the croft where my father was born, make up one thread that runs intermittently through the story and this is simply because the family information I had access to was particularly full and varied, and what happened there was fairly typical of what happened on holdings across the island.

Inevitably, there is a little overlap with my first book but not, I hope, too much. To it I must refer the reader for a much more detailed account of the late eighteenth and the nineteenth centuries, of the crofting economy that evolved and the problems it faced, of the island's church life and school, of the links of custom and kinship that bound the society together, both at home and in the emigrant communities overseas.

Again, my debts of thanks are many. Numerous people have been generous with information and memories but, had time permitted, I could have talked with many more. Iona has an astonishingly large adoptive population beyond its own shores. It has been possible to incorporate a great deal of the material gathered, but by no means all. Yet everything I have learned or heard from others has helped to fill in the background to events, or deepen my understanding of them, and for this I am grateful. Final responsibility for all errors of fact or interpretation, of course, rests with myself.

As before, my father, Dugald MacArthur, has been unfailingly supportive, and his wealth of knowledge about the island and its people has been indispensable. Both this book and its companion are, in a real sense, as much his as mine.

E.M.M.

Part One

An I mo chridhe, I mo ghràidh
In Iona of my heart, Iona of my love

1

The Island Now Called I-Colm Kill

Seachd bliadhna roimh 'n bhràth
Thig muir air Eirinn rè aon tràth
'S thar Ile ghuirm ghlais
Ach snàmhaidh I Choluim Chlèirich

The prophecy foretells that seven years before the day of judgement the ocean will sweep over both Ireland and Islay. Yet the isle of St Columba will swim above the waves.

Many drawn to Iona over the centuries have regarded the place, and the events that have happened there, as of enduring importance. The old saying echoes this sense of the eternal, this tendency to see the island as unchanging and indestructible.

Its very foundation stones command similar influence, even yet. Iona's basic landscape was formed of Lewisian gneiss, as old as any of the oldest rocks in Britain, and a layer of Torridonian sediment later settled along the eastern rim. It was still too early for any hard-shelled living creature to leave a trace of its existence. Along with changing climates over the millenia and the much later addition of shell sand, these formations helped determine what grew on the island and thus, eventually, its flower and plant life and its agriculture. They have ensured that to the traveller's eye Iona's mixture of grey and green and silvery white looks at once distinctive, whether approached from the dark basalt cliffs of Staffa and central Mull to the north or across the Ross of Mull's mass of red granite to the east.

3

Geological antiquity, moreover, has lent it added mystique for those of romantic bent, who have tended to describe this small place as springing from the moment when history began, as rising 'like the first draught of Creation' in the words of one nineteenth-century cleric. Many other tracts of Archaean gneiss are of equally venerable age. But they did not go on to form Iona, this island of less than six kilometres in length and barely two and a half wide. Even its rocks, it seems, have at times been given an exaggerated tale to tell.

Why and when did these particular rocks become so special? What they were first called ought to hold some clues but even this is obscure. The island has had a variety of names, the names have been spelled in different ways, and the spellings have been pored over by generations of scholars. Yet no one has ever been able to say with certainty: this is the true name of this place and this is what it means.

Many agree that 'Iona' probably resulted from a manuscript mis-reading of 'Ioua Insula' in Adomnán's *Life of Columba* and that the nominative form of the first word was 'Io' or 'I', equating with an old Gaelic word, possibly meaning territory or island. Place-name scholar W. J. Watson felt that this element was 'Iogh' signifying a yew tree. There have been unlikely sorties into the possibilities of 'isle of waves' – I-thonna – or 'happy isle' – I-shona – and much discussion about doves. Dean Monro, whose description of the island in 1549 is the earliest extant by an outside observer, gave its name as 'Sanct Colm's Ile' in English and 'Icholum chille' in Gaelic. Bishop Pococke, who visited in 1760, tried out a few variations: 'Hii or I or Y, that is the island now called I-Colm Kill'. For Gaels, over many centuries, this is the name by which the island has been known. A manuscript dated 1848, the earliest written account we have by an inhabitant in modern times, states that the local people had used 'I Chaluim Chille' in common conversation for generations. So for them it was simply the place of Colum of the cell or church.

To Colum Cille – or St Columba in his sanctified and Latinised form – this dot on the ocean owes its fame. The medieval and modern religious institutions for which Iona also became renowned followed in his train. According to Adomnán he bestowed a final blessing on the island, 'small and mean though it be', and predicted that 'great and especial honour' would be paid it by rulers and peoples both near and far. Colum Cille's influence on Iona was to be far-reaching, but he was not by any means the first to set foot on its shores.

From at least the middle of the fifth millenium BC small groups of hunter-gatherers stepped lightly from site to site, as the seasons turned, along the mainland and among the islands of what is today Argyll. Stone and antler tools, along with shells and bones from fish and mammals have been found in cave deposits around Oban, on an island in Loch Sunart, on Ulva to the north and on Oronsay to the south. The rocks of Iona will not have been as hospitable as some of these parts, until the sea level finally receded to leave a fertile raised beach, but a few unworked flints from the Mesolithic period have come to light during excavations near the cathedral complex.

Farming communities drifted in to the island from about BC 3500, as pollen analysis and the discovery of several worked flints have indicated. They seem to have been active along the eastern coast and in the vicinity of the Lochan Mòr below Dùn I. Early in the twentieth century, on the portion of land by then known as Clachanach, a sharpening stone and another for skinning were unearthed by chance in the course of digging, as were a few hazel nuts, knarled and brown, remnants from the woodland cover of those times.

From the Bronze Age, perhaps in the second millenium BC, only one burial cairn has been recorded on Iona although, from about the same time, quite a rich legacy of standing stones pepper the landscape of neighbouring Mull. There must have been some kind of a population to put them up, for whatever reasons now long obscured. Yet even those mysterious ancient monoliths have been pressed into service in relation to the smaller island. In the *Proceedings of the Society of Antiquaries of Scotland* for 1863 the Revd Thomas Maclaughlan claimed to have noted an entire series of standing stones leading along the Ross of Mull between Pennycross and Fionnphort. Upon enquiring of the local minister, the Revd Donald McVean of whom we shall hear more in due course, he found that 'tradition is uniform among the natives, that they were intended as guide-posts to strangers visiting Iona on pilgrimage'.

This rather assumes that there was already something worth visiting when they were first erected in the pre-Christian era and that enough pilgrims would choose a land rather than a sea route to make the exercise worthwhile. The idea of these dramatic megaliths as markers to a sacred destination has surfaced since, now and again, even though milestones of considerably more modest dimensions have served just as well on countless other routes. It is hard to avoid the conclusion that an extra reputation has been foisted upon the standing stones of Mull because of their proximity to Iona where, perhaps curiously, there appear to be none at all. Caution may be advisable on this point, however, since it is just possible that we may not have recognised their sites. They may have been incorporated into other structures or removed.

The Iron Age spans the point before and after which we have become used to measuring the centuries and sometime within about a hundred years BC and two hundred AD people occupied a small hill fort on Iona. You can climb there now, to the top of Dùn Bhuirg north-west of the Machair, and see a section of the rampart they built to defend their small community. From the careful scrapings of the archaeologists we know that they kept warm around a hearth in the centre of a stone-built hut, about four metres square; that they had pottery and fired clay vessels; and that they used the meat and skins of cattle and red deer, of pig and sheep and seal. One of them once wore or handled tiny yellow glass beads.

It is impossible to tell how long these fort-dwellers remained on Iona, or whether others succeeded them in or around their hill-top home, but it is entirely reasonable to speculate that some did so. On the eastern edge, too, archaeologists have found ample evidence of Iron Age activity. These people will have come, we must suppose, from the medley of northern tribes speaking a Celtic language whom the Romans had classed together conveniently as Picts.

They will have had beliefs and customs, as all peoples do. A little to the north of Dùn Bhuirg lies Dùn Mhanannain, its name commemorating a pagan god of the sea. A vestige of the ancient rite of casting oatmeal upon the waves, in return for the seaware cast up on the shore, was said to have remained on Iona as late as the eighteenth century. Witnessed about the same time too were remains of a structure – perhaps a stone circle – on top of Sìthean Mòr, the grassy knoll also visible across the Machair from Dùn Bhuirg. Here horses ran sunwise on the feast day of St Michael, stories of fairy music and dancing abounded and on the great quarterly festival of May Day, Làtha Bealltuinn, fires were said to be kindled on its summit and the cattle driven through in an act of purification. And this spot's alternative name Cnoc nan Aingeal or Hill of the Angels, linked to it by the legend that Colum Cille saw a heavenly vision there, is given another inter-pretation in an eighteenth-century manuscript description of the Beltane ceremonies: 'One of the highest [round hills] and most cen-trical in Icolmkill is called Cnoc-nan-Ainneal, ie the hill of the fires.' The Gaelic word 'aingeal' can indeed mean both angel and fire.

Such rituals were not of course exclusive to Iona but formed part of a general body of lore and belief alive throughout the Celtic world in pre-Christian times. It is well attested that the new faith tackled some of the older practices by absorbing and adapting them, taking over pagan festival dates for example or giving saints' names to sacred wells. But one would be mistaken to see the two creeds merging smoothly into some gentle, nature-loving whole, for the first missionaries strong-ly condemned much of what they encountered. Discussing this in rela-tion to St Patrick in their history of the early Irish church, Walsh and Bradley make an intriguing suggestion about the oft-quoted passage where Colum Cille cares for a wounded crane. A humane action, cer-tainly, but was it also a clear hint that this man of God would have no truck with the old Celtic view of the crane as a bird of evil portent?

So, was there in fact an established community of sun-worshippers on Iona when Colum Cille arrived, and was it his first dramatic task to drive them out? This became a picture beloved of much popular travel writing of the nineteenth century, by which time the references in classical literature to Druids – priests and divinators of some kind among the Celtic tribes – had been elaborated into a largely fanciful cult. Conveniently, yet another name for Iona was 'Innis nan Druidh-neach', usually translated as Isle of Druids. Others countered with the explanation, just as plausible, that the word was properly 'Druinneach' meaning sculptor or craftsman and dated from the period when the island's school of carving was at the height of its fame. A burial ground named Cladh nan Druinneach, just south-west of Martyrs Bay and enclosed until last century, might very possibly have been set aside for these men since different cemeteries for different purposes were not uncommon in medieval times.

Without doubt people had come and gone from Iona more or less continuously over a few thousand years in pre-Columban times. As Dean Monro was to observe a thousand years after that, this was 'ane faire mayne ile ... fruitful of corne and store and guid for fishing'. Not enough had changed, in climate or topography, to make this substantially less true for the sixth century as for the sixteenth. It was an attractive place to settle. Whether any who did were of special significance, thus already transferring special qualities to the island, is a case whose verdict must remain not proven.

2

A Man of Blessed Memory

A lengthy and tortuous exchange of correspondence in the *Oban Times* during the summer of 1919, about whether the Columban church was Roman or Celtic, produced a sceptical rejoinder at one point: 'So little is known about St Columba that we should receive everything we hear and read concerning him with a large lump of salt.' It is easy to feel similarly bewildered when faced with so much ingenious rehashing, over so long a time, of so few hard facts. Yet the simple truth that he has merited such a huge degree of interest down the ages signals the importance of this man, of what he did and of what he inspired in others.

Thanks to St Columba the island of Iona has been called the 'cradle' of Christianity in Scotland, a strangely inaccurate description for one so often repeated. As receptacle for a new-born infant, prior claim must of course be made by Whithorn where the elusive Ninian laboured among a colony Christianised at least a century earlier. And if the purpose of a cradle is to induce a state of peaceful somnolence, then the circumstances surrounding Colum Cille's arrival on Iona appear to have been anything but sleepy. Violent struggle played some part in both halves of Dál Riata, kingdom of the Scots who, in the course of the fifth century, had seeped steadily over from what is now the Antrim coast to modern-day Kintyre and south Argyll.

The saint was born in Donegal in 521 into the Cenél Conaill – one of the royal households of the day – but, apart from the fact that he studied for the monastic life under various teachers, even less is documented for the forty or so years before he left Ireland than for those that followed. In the year 561 his family fought in the bloody battle of Cúl Dreimne and Colum Cille himself appears to have been implicated, directly or indirectly. Whether he was banished shortly after this or went into self-imposed exile as a penance or set sail with the conscious aim of winning over barbarous hordes beyond the horizon, we do not know for certain.

What he almost certainly and very sensibly did do first was visit one of his relations – Conall, king of the Dál Riatan Scots. Depending on which chronicler you follow, it was either Conall who gifted Iona to him as a base or it was Brude, king of the northern Picts. Scholars concur, however, that there may be an element of truth in both accounts. The island lay near the farthest edge of the Dál Riatan territory and it may well be that Scots had already established a foothold there with a small settlement. Indeed, one wonders how Conall could have been confident in granting it to anyone were this not the case.

Nor is the question of who held sovereignty over neighbouring Mull entirely clear, but cairns – reputedly ancient – on the hills to either side of Glen More are named Càrn Cùl ri Albainn and Càrn Cùl ri Eirinn. These are traditionally believed to mean cairns of the back to, respectively, Alba or Pictland and Ireland or Dál Riata. Local lore of more recent vintage, but presumably echoing some kind of notion that this was once a borderland, points to the Clach Mhollach and the Clach Bhiorach as markers of the old line between the kingdoms of the Picts and Scots. These two large boulders, one round-topped and tufted with heather and one sharply pointed, can still be seen by the old road through the Glen. The two hills also named Càrn Cùl ri Eirinn, one in Oronsay and one in Iona itself, may also have been demarcation points as the Scots pushed their territory northwards.

In 560, however, just three years before the date generally accepted for the foundation at Iona, the Picts had inflicted a serious defeat on the Scots. It would have been wise to negotiate with these inflammable neighbours before launching in among them with a new religion. It is therefore quite likely that the famous journey through the Great Glen to the court of King Brude, undertaken soon after Colum Cille's arrival, had a primarily diplomatic rather than an evangelistic motive.

Iona was a practical and strategic spot. Besides its good natural attributes, it lay at the centre of the waterways which linked the Irish and Scottish Dál Riata to the northern area their rulers wished to conquer or convert. Some months, maybe even years, after their departure from Ireland and somewhere near the burn that runs across the grassy slopes of the island's north-east side, Colum Cille and his companions built a small monastery of wood, wattle and daub. All that may be seen today are traces of the vallum, the raised earth boundary that enclosed it.

Most of what we know of this the first recorded religious foundation on Iona comes from Adomnán, abbot during the last two decades of the seventh century. A little may also be gleaned from Irish annals and from the English chronicler Bede, writing around the year 730. Although Adomnán's *Life of Columba* dates from a century after the saint's death, it incorporates material from another *Life* – now lost – written by his predecessor, Abbot Cumméne. These were not biographies in the sense that this word is understood today, but set out to demonstrate qualities of saintliness in their subject through the recounting of prophecies, divine visions and miracles. 'There was a man of venerable life and blessed memory, the father and founder of monasteries ...' begins Adomnán's second preface.

The value of Adomnán's *Life of Columba* has been dismissed by some writers in the past as too devoid of historical fact to be of much use. Fortunately it has been assessed thoughtfully by many more, for example in the mid-nineteenth century edition by Irish clergyman William Reeves and through the outstanding scholarship of Alan O. Anderson and Marjorie O. Anderson, whose translation and commentary on the *Life* has recently been republished.

Helpful too is the overview of the times by Alfred Smyth in his *Warlords and Holy Men*. He reminds us of the contemporary crises in which both abbots were writing: Cumméne soon after the setback of the Synod of Whitby which decided in favour of certain practices following Roman rather than Celtic usage; and Adomnán amid continuing controversy on Iona over these same questions. He had been persuaded to move into line with the Northumbrian church by adopting Roman ways but had not been able to bring his own community with him. It may thus have seemed necessary to reaffirm the principles of a simple spiritual life, whose superior was God rather than any one particular Church authority, and which could best be exemplified through the person of Iona's founder. If a counterblast was ever considered, an alternative view of the saint's thoughts and deeds, then it has not come down to us. Even if it had, that too would certainly have to be treated with similar caution and not accepted automatically as hard, objective evidence.

Adomnán's *Life* does, however, contain a wealth of small but vivid detail about the monastic way of life from Colum Cille's day up to and beyond his own. And there is no reason to doubt that the traits of personality revealed through fabulous or mystical episodes bore genuine relation to those of the saint himself. Smyth points out that the nine abbots up to and including Adomnán were, with one exception, of the same kin and this will have reinforced the strong tradition, which undoubtedly existed, of passing down information and stories by word of mouth through the 'family' of monks.

Again, archaeological and place-name evidence have helped fill out Adomnán's picture of life on Iona during the sixth and seventh centuries. The monks planted crops, probably barley, and harvested them around their enclosure and on the 'western plain' which we now call the Machair. They slept in single cells but ate together in the refectory, their diet consisting chiefly of bread, eggs, fish, shellfish, milk and some meat, particularly from cattle but to a lesser degree also from sheep, pigs and deer. They seem to have used a breeding colony of seals on a nearby island, possibly Soa or Erraid, for food and skins. Some of the monks developed particular skills, as blacksmiths to forge iron tools, as metal- and glassworkers, woodturners and shoemakers.

Somewhere along Sruth a' Mhuilinn was the mill after which the burn was named, probably of the small horizontal kind, although the earliest monks may have used querns to grind their grain by hand. There was a granary and a kiln. As late as 1920 the then parish minister, an enthusiast for Iona's history, could identify remains of a kiln beside the burn but it would be impossible to claim this as dating from the Columban monastery. Kilns, vital for drying out grain before grinding and of which there were probably several at various periods, were also used by the medieval abbey and by the local population. Traces of another one can still be seen from the road about half a kilometre to the north, in a field below Dùn I.

Excavations in 1991 found a man-made pool cutting across the present course of the burn and a group of large post-pits at the downstream end of the area. This has been tentatively suggested as the undercroft of a mill, probably timber-built but, again, this is likely to have been working in or up until the relatively modern era of two hundred years ago. Many traditional activities recur down the ages in the same areas, however, for the simple reason that these remain the best and most suitable sites.

When not labouring to feed and house themselves, the monks devoted their time to study and prayer, to the writing of annals, to the copying and illuminating of the psalter and the gospels. The moving account of Colum Cille's last hours includes an image of him at work in his hut, bent over a transcription of the thirty-third psalm.

Particular sounds were introduced into the environment, as small iron hand-bells summonsed the brethern to their small oratory for divine office several times during the day and night. Not that we should assume by any means that the landscape had for ever been silent, save for birdsong. Early inhabitants may have had the horns and rattles that existed in the Bronze Age. The late John MacMillan told the author that near Port a' Churaich he was once shown a ringing rock, one of our most ancient instruments for sounding a resonant signal. And there is another such rock just north of Port na Fraing on the east coast.

Now monks' voices rose and fell in the chanting of the psalms, an integral part of their worship and a musical form of peculiar beauty that was to spread with the Christian faith throughout Europe. In his seminal work on the music of Scotland, John Purser describes 'the only definitive remnants of the music of the Celtic church' as contained in the *Inchcolm Antiphoner*. This precious manuscript dates from around the very end of the thirteenth century and clearly has some close link with Inchcolm Priory, founded early in the twelfth century and dedicated to St Columba. Indeed, Inchcolm has been called 'the Iona of the East'. The texts within the *Antiphoner* which mention St Columba are unique in the known body of plainchant and, from a study of the verse and melody structures, Purser believes their origin could be as early as

the seventh to ninth centuries. It is not impossible that they, or chants
very like them, were sung on Iona.

This Early Christian community will have been close-knit and dedicated to its chosen life but there were also those who wished to be
alone, as a few clues on the surface of the land outside of the vallum tell
us. In a dent in the hills to the south-west of Dùn I lie the remains of a
circular stone hut, popularly known as the Hermit's or Culdee Cell.
The latter term is a corruption of the Gaelic name recorded by Reeves
in 1857, Cobhan Cùilteach, which simply means 'secluded hollow'.
Was this place used for solitary contemplation? Those who believe it
was sometimes link it to Iomaire Tochair, an artificial embankment
leading from the vallum north-west across the Lochan Mòr. This in
turn has been associated with Cilline Droichteach who succeeded as
abbot in the first half of the eighth century and whose name means
'bridge-builder'. He is thought to have been the first anchorite, or
recluse, to hold the office and it has thus been tempting to suppose that
he made a causeway across the end of the loch for easier access to the
hut he, or a predecessor, had built.

There are still a good few hundred metres between the end of the
Iomaire and Cobhan Cùilteach, however. And it is hard to imagine that
the monks, or any settlers, will not have been adept at finding the
driest and most direct tracks over the moors long before Cilline
Droichteach's day. An alternative school of thought identifies the
causeway as a dam, perhaps related to the mill burn. And archaeologist
John Barber wonders if it may have served to create a water-meadow,
whereby grass continued to grow all winter under the surface of a
flooded and frozen area of pasture. This was then drained to provide
lush, early grazing in the first days of spring. It is an intriguing interpretation. After all, relating everything primarily to the monks'
spiritual life diverts attention from the fact that they also had to survive.
They are bound to have managed the resources of the land in appropriate, and no doubt ingenious, ways.

This constant need to tend and provide for cattle brings us back
to the 'cell' in Cobhan Cùilteach. It was certainly made by someone
for some reason, and traces of what may be a track leading from it
to the south-east are faintly discernable even yet. It is the build-up of

tradition, however, rather than firm archaeological or place-name evidence, that has bestowed on this particular site a solely religious role. There are several other stone foundations scattered around the island, of similar or smaller size, some of which may have been temporary dwellings at some period but which also undoubtedly served as shelter for herds, for milking cows out on the common pasture or for holding a calf apart from its mother. The Cobhan Cùilteach itself may easily have been reused by the islanders for these purposes, especially as a stock enclosure of fairly modern date has been built against a nearby cliff-face.

A vivid reminder of this possibility comes from two islanders whose grandmother expressed a wish to see the 'Hermit's Cell' of which the visitors talked so much. They walked the old lady out there, across the hummocks and boggy hollows, and her reaction was both spontaneous and down to earth: 'But this is just like the circles where we milked the cows in the West End hills when I was young!' So it was. She was growing up on Iona in the 1890s when this practice was still common.

Again, a little documentary evidence comes together with remains on the ground at Cladh an Diseirt, the burial place of the hermitage, near to the bay of the same name. Reeves's map, using local knowledge from the mid-nineteenth century, also includes the word 'Leacht' below the name. This is presumably 'leac' meaning a tombstone.

Up until the late 1860s, when James Drummond made a sketch, a lintel crowned the two granite pillars still there today, to give the impression of a gateway. Pococke also noted these stones in 1760 but took them to be the remains of 'a Druid temple'. Could this indeed, just possibly, have been where a group of pre-Christian standing stones was built into a cell or small oratory? This is not the only question left unanswered, nor the only instance of speculation fuelled by human imagination.

A reference in the *Annals of Ulster* from 1164 includes the name MacGilladuib as head of the 'disertach' at Iona, and one interpretation is that the small chapel there dates from the twelfth century, serving some section of the then monastic community at a discreet distance from the main settlement. It was perhaps dedicated to St John because of the persistence of a second name for it, Cladh Iain – burial place of John.

The lingering idea that the site may in fact go back much further, to Early Christian times, cannot be proved without proper excavation. The notion was bumped into life by a crofter's cartwheel about 1870. Dugald MacArthur regularly carted seaweed for his fields at Clachanach from Port an Diseirt, along a track he had made himself that ran north past the burial place. Each time he felt the jolt over one particular stone just protruding out of the earth near to the north-east corner. Eventually he dug it up. Almost oval in shape, it had a ringed cross on one side and so he left it for safe-keeping on top of the large boulder in the field above. He told the minister Alexander MacGregor about it, who in due course informed the antiquarian William Skene. Eventually it was placed along with other carved stones within the cathedral precincts.

But was it significant? Skene and Drummond examined the site in 1876, finding a cross-fragment now impossible to identify, and speculated that the oval stone may have marked a grave. Adomnán's *Life* states that when the saint died, the stone upon which he had rested his head in sleep was turned into a monument at the spot where he was buried. Skene became convinced that this was here, at Cladh an Diseirt, and that the little chapel at the cathedral's west end – known as St Columba's Cell – housed the saint's enshrined bones only, and not his body, during a later period. Whatever the true story below those grassy humps close to the shore, the little stone that came to light by chance has ever since been firmly labelled 'St Columba's Pillow'.

At no stage in Iona's history will it have been possible to deny the power and presence of the sea. Today, dominated as we are by over-land communications, it is easy to forget that for centuries Scotland's west coast was a busy maritime thoroughfare. In Colum Cille's time, and as the reputation of his monastery strengthened over succeeding generations, the sea carried a steady stream of pilgrims seeking teaching, healing or absolution. It brought exiles such as Oswald, a prince of Northumbria who sought refuge among the Scots during a time of turmoil and became a convert. When he later gained his throne in 634 he sought a missionary from the Celtic church and so the great centre at Lindisfarne, under Aidan from Iona, was born.

The waters cast up strays from time to time, for example the shipwrecked Arculf who found himself on Iona for a spell during Adomnán's abbacy. The misfortune that threw together this Gaulish bishop and the scholarly island abbot has left Dark Age historians with a rare bonus, Adomnán's book *The Holy Places*. For Arculf had just travelled through the Holy Land and was able to give his eager listener an eyewitness account of what the countries and cities of the Near East looked like, along with myriad details about their social, political and religious conditions. In a wattle cell amid the Hebrides, the Gael and the Gaul talked of the Sea of Galilee, of crocodiles on the Nile, of an icon of the Virgin Mary in Constantinople.

The ocean brought danger too, however. Before the end of the eighth century the Vikings had swept down the west coast for the first time, plundering and killing. The island monastery was a defenceless target and in 807 Abbot Cellach retreated to Ireland to build a new foundation for his monks at Kells. A small community did hold on in Iona. Indeed, the writing of a ninth-century German abbot, Walafrid Strabo, implies that an Irish monk named Blathmac deliberately sought out the island where 'many a pagan horde of Danes is wont to land' and was slain there in the year 825. 'Thus Blathmac became a martyr for Christ's name' concludes the chronicle, provoking the image of Iona, even then, as a place where it was not only saintly to live and work but also to die.

The island remained exposed to attack and in 849 the relics of Colum Cille were divided, to be taken to Kells in Ireland and to a church founded by Kenneth MacAlpin, probably at Dunkeld. The wave of raids on Iona came to an end with the slaughter, on Christmas Eve 986, of the abbot and fifteen monks. By then, the early timber monastery had been rebuilt in stone, and foundations excavated in 1957 below the present cathedral cloister garth have been tentatively identified as belonging to this period. Ian Cowie, a member of the Iona Community, has never forgotten watching the archaeologists at work one summer day at the south-east corner of the cloisters as, out into the twentieth-century light, there emerged a skull. Then came several more plus the entire skeletons of seven or eight men. They had died violently. One had his pinkie clamped between his teeth.

Slightly concerned that the young son by his side might be frightened at such a grisly sight, Ian asked if he was all right. A child's curiosity still had the upper hand, however, as the boy replied without alarm: 'I suppose that's what you call a skullery!' It is not impossible that the 'skullery' was once the chapel where those monks were at prayer, for the last time, that December night in 986. Their remains were given a respectful reburial in the cathedral grounds.

The Columban monks changed Iona physically, to a degree. Or at least they accelerated a process previous inhabitants had begun, by clearing oak and ash trees for their timber needs and making inroads into the remaining natural scrub of birch, willow, hazel and rowan. There are virtually no old indigenous trees there today. What their monastery and mission set in motion also changed the island in a less tangible, but equally permanent, way. It became 'The Sacred Isle', perceived as such throughout the lands which eventually became Scotland and beyond. It could no longer be just one Hebridean island among many. The prince and priest Colum Cille, and by extension Iona itself, have ever since been bound into the national story.

3

The Legacy of Colum Cille

The authority of Iona's founding father was high enough, spiritually and politically, for him to ordain Aedán King of Dál Riata in 574. According to Adomnán, Aedán went to the island for that purpose. The saint's associations with royalty, and with the warring that attended struggles for power, remained strong long after his death. Items associated with the saint were carried before armies – an enshrined psalter in Ireland, a crozier in Scotland. The Breccbennach is said to have been paraded before the Scots, to hearten them, before the battle of Bannockburn even though this tiny, delicately ornamented casket was by then probably empty. But it had once held a relic of Colum Cille. It now sits in the National Museum of Scotland, as the Monymusk Reliquary, an exquisite national treasure.

That an object of beauty be closely identified with a leader of the Celtic church evokes no surprise. Iona is one of the places which bears witness to the extraordinary artistic heritage these early generations of monks bequeathed. The magnificent *Book of Kells* was in all probability begun here, before its removal to Ireland for safety during the perilous ninth century. The Early Christian incised stones and high crosses still on the island form one of the country's outstanding collections. All of this creative activity shows signs of cross-fertilisation with Ireland, across to Northumbria and north through the Great Glen to the heart of Pictland. Missionary monks travelled, and their ideas journeyed with them. In due course, late medieval craftsmen were to add to Iona's storehouse of riches with their intricately carved grave-slabs and splendid effigies of leading figures from the West Highland aristocracy.

There will at one time have been more standing crosses than those in existence today. Fragments and bases of some have survived as have references to two in particular, named after St Brandon and St Adomnán. On his map published in 1928 Alex Ritchie, who had access to much local place-name knowledge, gives Port Adomnán and Port a' Chroisein – bay of the little cross – as alternative names for part of the shore below the village. Two other places known in oral tradition imply the presence of crosses: Parc nan Croisean just south of the St Columba Hotel, and Na Croisean Mòra between the road north of the cathedral and the vallum. It was customary in early monastic times to erect a cross, perhaps a simple one of wood or unadorned stone, at the spot where an event of significance occurred and Adomnán does imply that this happened on Iona.

That there were ever as many as 360 standing crosses, however, sub-sequently thrown down by frenzied Church reformers in the sixteenth century is highly unlikely. The evidence for and against this was weighed in an article by J. R. N. MacPhail for the *Scottish Historical Review* of 1925. He pointed out that the figure must derive from a conflation of two remarks made by William Sacheverell, governor of Man, who visited Iona in 1688. These were, first, that a note of 300 stones with *inscriptions* was in the possession of the Revd Farquhar Fraser, dean of the Isles from 1633 to 1680, and secondly that the Synod of Argyll allegedly ordered 60 crosses to be cast into the sea.

An act was indeed passed by the General Assembly of 1640 that 'idolatrous monuments' be demolished, especially in the north of Scotland, and there was subsequently an expedition through the isles for that purpose led by the Marquess of Argyll. He did create a degree of havoc, overturning 'all crosses and memorials of the saints' he could find, according to a contemporary account. In Iona he made an unsuc-cessful effort to appropriate the great cathedral bell but, although a few crosses may have been broken, those we see today were left standing as was the earlier marble altar. The shorthand of '360 crosses de-stroyed' crept into print astonishingly quickly. Dean Fraser's own son John included it in his reply to Sir Robert Sibbald, seeking material for

MacFarlane's Geographical Collections of 1693. It has been repeated time and again ever since.

One effect of the Columban mission's activity that is clearer than the fate of the crosses, and was almost as far-reaching as its spiritual influence, is its linguistic and literary legacy. Although familiar with Latin for worship and writing, the monks spoke Gaelic. An early eighteenth-century Mull bard, the Revd John Maclean, referred eloquently to these roots in verses that lamented the decline of his language:

> Si labhair Padric 'nnínse Fail na Riogh
> 'San faighe caomhsin, Colum náomhtha 'n I.

> It was Gaelic that Patrick spoke in Inse Fail of the kings
> As did that gentle prophet, the holy Colum, in Iona.

Sooner or later that form of Celtic tongue brought from Ireland would presumably have spread out from its foothold in Argyll, in step with the Scots' expanding territory. But its inextricable link with the powerful faith that was pushing northward, and the authority imbued in it through the person of Colum Cille himself, ensured that the language took root earlier and more widely than it might have done.

The monks were also learned and literate men to whom we owe some of our earliest written texts. Adomnán has left us the country's oldest hagiography. From a Celtic monastic foundation in Aberdeenshire comes the *Book of Deer* in which the Latin manuscript, dating from about the ninth century, is supplemented by Gaelic notes written into the margins about three hundred years later. These form the oldest surviving examples of Scottish Gaelic prose. And earliest of all is the 'Amra Choluim Chille'. This vernacular praise poem about the saint, in his native language, is thought to have been composed soon after his death, about the beginning of the seventh century.

Although Colum Cille is revered as the outstanding figure in the early Celtic church he was not of course alone. Much too was achieved through the foundations of contemporaries, among them Brendan of Clonfert on Tiree and possibly also in the Garvellochs, Donnán on Eigg and Moluag on Lismore. The first Iona monastery also founded a daughter house on Tiree along with others on Loch Awe side and on the unidentified islands of 'Elan' and 'Hinba'. The saint seems to have spent a lot of time on Hinba, which some have believed to be Jura although more incline towards Eileach an Naoimh in the Garvellochs. Dr John Lorne Campbell makes a persuasive claim that it was Canna, where a chapel is dedicated to Colum Cille.

The Iona monastery's founder was also its abbot, the holder of an office which laid upon him considerable spiritual and administrative responsibilities and conflicts slightly with the role of missionary into which he has been popularly moulded, roaming ever farther into the unenlightened realms of Pictland. Adomnán does indicate two visits to Skye but most scholars agree that mass conversion of the Picts by Colum Cille directly is not supported by the evidence. It would be the missions of Adomnán himself, and the work of Maelrubha from Applecross more than a century later, that were to make the real impact on the heathen north-west.

For the achievements of that first small settlement on Iona cannot be isolated from the Irish context in which it was rooted nor from all the activity, in a variety of directions, which sprang up in its wake. The Christianising of Northumbria was of huge significance and can certainly be traced directly to Iona's influence. From within the broader Celtic church monks reached out across Europe, notably Columbanus who worked tirelessly in eastern France, Switzerland and Italy.

And Alfred Smyth has argued that Iona's early pre-eminent position has rendered it even more important for today's students of the period, since it resulted in a rich vein of documentary references to what was happening there. These come both from outside chroniclers who recognised the island's status and indirectly from the monks themselves who, it is thought, almost certainly compiled the originals from which some of the extant Irish annals were copied. Thus we have been left a crucial key to understanding how the early Church was organised, how its abbacy was passed on and how it related to the political powers of the day.

Guidebooks have tended to assert that Iona's saint set up, in his lifetime, at least a hundred churches in Scotland and personally converted thousands. This would have been good going even for one who lived into his seventies, which was a relatively advanced age for those times. The evidence indicates that Colum Cille did not travel as far outside of the Scottish Dál Riatan lands as is often assumed, although he did return to Ireland at least twice. Yet this does not necessarily diminish his stature nor invalidate the widespread adoption of his name into church dedications, into place-names and into general lore.

How the cult of the saint evolved on the island itself, and through whom, is an interesting question. When Martin Martin visited Iona about 1695 and mentioned to the natives the tradition that Colum Cille was buried in Ireland, they were most indignant 'and affirmed that the Irish who said so were impudent liars'. In 1764 Dr John Walker gained the impression that 'every person has the traditional history of Columba with numberless legends, which have been handed down from his monkish seminary'.

We cannot tell for certain when a secular population sprang up alongside the very first monastery. But it is likely that one did so fairly soon, made up perhaps of pilgrims or travellers who stayed on, and whoever may have already been on the island. In the early medieval period, the Benedictine monks and Augustinian nuns will have had servants to help work the land, or lay brethren brought in for particular kinds of labour. And the families in ascendancy in the Mull area at various times may have moved their kindred into Iona – and out again, as fortunes changed.

Thus any attempt to prove that a coherent body of lore about Iona's first famous inhabitant was passed directly down the ages on the island itself would be fraught with difficulties. Over the centuries, between the early Irish settlements and the visits of Martin and Walker, the local population will have been infused with new blood, perhaps several times. Yet those who came in will have been Gaels, from the Irish and then increasingly from the Scottish Gaidhealtachd. And the name of Colum Cille, which spread widely and swiftly as the prestige of Iona grew, will have been very familiar to them and become, to some degree, bound into their prayers and proverbs and legendary stories. In Alexander Carmichael's great nineteenth-century collection of verse, charms and incantations, published under the title of *Carmina Gadelica*, the name of Colum Cille predominates. This work has to be interpreted with care, however, as Carmichael undoubtedly edited and reassembled much of the material, and although it does tap into an older vein of oral tradition, the original emphases may have become obscured by his day.

Some of the lore that washed in and out of Iona had taken strange side-steps or become mingled with ancient superstition. A Gaelic proverb attached itself to Colum Cille at some point and stuck there: 'Far am bi bò bi bean agus far am bi bean bi buaireadh; Where there is a cow there is a woman and where there is a woman there is mischief'. The eminent good sense of the first phrase is usually overlooked. Milking and tending cattle have for a very long time been traditionally female occupations in the Highlands. The saying has been taken to mean that the saint banished both species to the conveniently named Eilean nam Ban – the island of women – close to the Ross of Mull coast.

Yet no other mysoginist tendencies on Colum Cille's part have come down to us. Indeed, he is credited with helping a woman in labour in one of his miracles. And how then did the monks get their milk every day, across a frequently choppy mile of open water? It rather contradicts, too, one of the most frequently quoted passages from Adomnán where a white horse, 'used to carry milk pails between the cattle pasture and the monastery', was blessed by the saint in the last hours of his life.

Eilean nam Ban, which is documented as early as Blaeu's map of 1662, will have received its name for some reason, however. An intriguing explanation comes from an unpublished manuscript, written in 1848 by Angus Lamont who was a local guide for many years. He states that while the nunnery was being built, a temporary dwelling housed the nuns over on that island and that nearby land was allocated to them to provide food. He even cites another saying: 'Na Fiddin, Salchur is Creich dhubh nan cailleach, tri bailltean as miosa ann an Muile a dhuinne dhol a shireadh bonaich; Fidden, Salchur and Creich of the nuns, the three worst farms in Mull for a person to seek food in'. Henry D. Graham, who was staying on Iona throughout the year in which Lamont wrote down his account, notes that former traces of habitation on Eilean nam Ban had lately disappeared. A footnote in Reeves (1857) repeats this – and specifically refers to these remains as 'a building called the Nunnery'. The idea clearly lingered on until at least 1899 when members of the Royal Society of Antiquaries in Ireland, on a visit to Iona, were informed that: 'A more ancient nunnery is said to have existed on the little island called Eilean nam

Ban ... and on which, some years since, there were traces of a building called by the country people the Nunnery.'

Early travellers were consistently told that stone from the cathedral and nunnery buildings came from Eilean nam Ban and quarrying marks are visible around much of the small island's coast. There would thus have been boats going to and fro during this period of its alleged occupation by the sisters. From the sea it looks quite forbidding, little more than a bare lump of granite. But the coastal rocks conceal a grassy sheltered strath, bright with wild flowers in summer, and there is at least one spring of fresh water. It is now unlikely we will know who the women were who drank from it or if any ever did at all.

In her *Folklore of the Scottish Highlands,* Dr Anne Ross advances the suggestion that an island of womenfolk might echo an old pagan legend about similar places, where human sacrifice was part of the rite. She raises this after discussing another legend closely associated with Iona, that of Odhrán who was said to have been buried alive to prevent the walls of the first church falling down. Odhrán, or St Oran in his English form, is thought to have been a cousin or contemporary of Colum Cille but Adomnán makes no mention of him or of any such event. Yet the story was widely known in the Highlands and Islands and seems to reflect that interweaving of pre- and post-Christian belief that underlies much of Gaelic tradition.

The Reilig Odhráin, the cemetery which commemorates the mysterious Odhrán, is another place where as many questions as answers arise. The word 'reilig' is thought by some to be a Gaelicised form of the Latin 'reliquiae', indicating remains or relics of significance. The eminent Dublin scholar Dr Todd, in notes made on a visit to Iona in 1851, stated that the word 'reilig' was frequently used in Ireland for a Church served by priests living under a rule or 'regula', as distinct from secular priests, and added: 'I have no doubt that the term Reilig Odhráin was originally the name of the chapel not of the burying place round it.' John MacCormick from the Ross of Mull, writing for the *Oban Times* in 1903, refers to the 'Rolaig' Odhráin which he stated was the local pronunciation. Dwelly's Gaelic dictionary does give 'rolaig' as a variant denoting one single grave.

But whose relics or whose grave? It was customary for monks to be buried within their precincts and close to where their founder had been laid. Excavation has confirmed several early travellers' reports that areas close to the present cathedral buildings do contain graves, although these might be from the later Columban and the medieval Benedictine period. Exactly where Colum Cille himself lived, worshipped and was buried, and his brethern after him, remains subject to speculation. In respect of his grave site, a measure of tradition and some architectural evidence of an early Christian date have come down in favour of the tiny chapel jutting out just north of the cathedral's west door, but this is not absolutely conclusive.

Meanwhile, at some point and for some reason, a piece of ground a short distance away became the most hallowed of soil in this already holy island. Between the ninth and the eleventh centuries the reputation of the Reilig Odhráin was of the highest order, that of a royal burial ground. To what extent it was *actually* used as such is open to doubt. The precise figures of 48 Scottish kings, 8 Norwegian and 4 Irish were quoted by Dean Monro in his *Western Isles of Scotland* of 1549 and have been repeated by numerous subsequent travellers and guidebooks. George Buchanan's Latin *History of Scotland* drew substantially on Monro's account of the Hebrides, and the earlier work was thus very influential.

Monro's own words, however, are illuminating. He described three 'tombs of stanes formit like little chapellis', each with a Latin inscription. That in the centre read 'Tumulus Regum Scotiae' and those on either side were for the kings of 'Hiberniae' and 'Norvegiae'. He did not say that any figures were inscribed on these chapel-like structures, nor had he counted any stones lying within them. His information on the numbers buried was 'according to our Scottis and Irish Chronicles'.

In other words, he was relying on basically the same material available to us today – medieval chronicles and a series of king lists, not all in agreement with each other and all copied from original sources now lost, although one cannot rule out the possibility that he had access to something no longer in existence. These documents have to be treated with circumspection, not only because of the simple possibility of error or duplication in transcription but because of the propagandist elements they might very well contain.

For example, it is recorded in one of the chronicles of the kings of

Scotland for the year 858 that 'Kenneth, Alpin's son, reigned over the Scots for sixteen years after destroying the Picts; and he died in Forteviot and was buried in the island of Iona where the three sons of Erc (Fergus, Loarn and Angus) were buried.' This last reference to the Irish Dál Riatan household which first claimed a foothold in Kintyre and Argyll is almost certainly the source for later assertions that Iona was a sacred resting-place of kings even before 563 AD. Fergus was three generations before Aedán, his great-grandson crowned in 574. It is now generally accepted by scholars that the Picts were not in fact destroyed outright, and that Kenneth was not the first to be king of both Picts and Scots. But he did come to be regarded as the founder of the ruling dynasty of a unified Scotland. Thus, if it was important for the chronicler to boost Kenneth MacAlpin's credentials as 'conqueror' of the Picts, then what better way than to link him in death to the earliest Scottish dynasty possible?

Jumping forward to the last annal entry of this kind, questions of a similar nature arise. In 1097 Donald Bane, son of Duncan, was buried at Dunkeld but 'his bones were removed thence to Iona'. Donald's various and vigorous reactions against encroaching Anglo-Norman influence in Scotland earned him regard as the last of the truly Celtic kings. Identifying his remains with the well-spring of the Celtic church might have been a means of reaffirming that reputation.

How many kings were brought to Iona, and exactly who they were, is now impossible to verify. No grave-slabs can be accurately identified for any of them, with the exception of the shadowy 'King of France'. Some sources claim he had come to the island after abdicating the throne. Angus Lamont relays what must have been a local tradition, that he was a French prince who died while visiting 'Lord MacDonald's house' and had requested that his remains be taken to Iona. To him is attached a stone very different from the rest, a slab of unpolished pink granite incised with a single cross. It lies in the Reilig Odhráin yet, as enigmatic as the legend enfolding it.

Nevertheless, there is no reason to suggest that Dean Monro invented the tombs he recorded. Martin, at the end of the seventeenth century, described them as shrines but the inscriptions had worn off. By the time of Pennant's visit in 1772 there were only 'slight remains that were built in a ridged form and arched within'. They may have

been rounded, cell-like shelters, perhaps simply built and prone to
dilapidation over the centuries. A number of early Dál Riatan kings,
both Scottish and Irish, were very probably buried there as, quite
feasibly, were a few Norse rulers within whose island territories Iona
lay from the end of the eleventh century until 1266. Monro also noted
the large number of graves for West Highland chiefs and their families.
His conclusion was simple. They were there because 'it wes the maist
honorable and ancient place that wes in Scotland in those days, as we
reid'.

The sheer weight of tradition built around the idea extends to the
funeral journeys. Places associated with the routes taken include
Corpach at the head of Loch Linnhe, Creag nam Marbh on Loch
Feochan south of Oban and, opposite it, Port nam Marbh on Loch
Spelve in Mull. These last two mean the rock and the bay of the dead
respectively. On the west coast of Jura there is Uamh Muinntir I, the
cave of the people of Iona and at the tip of the Ross of Mull there is
another cave, Uamh nam Marbh. If the sea was too rough for crossing,
coffins were laid to wait in this small round cave cut into the cliffside.
It is certainly chilly enough inside to believe that.

Upon touching land in Iona at Port nam Mairtear, coffins were
rested on the Ealadh, a smooth grassy mound at its head, before being
borne along Sraid nam Marbh – the street of the dead – to their final
destination. Port nam Mairtear is translated now as 'Martyrs Bay' and
popularly assumed to have been the site of a Viking massacre. But this
may well be a later association, because of the English name. A book
by parish minister Archibald MacMillan, published in 1898, suggests
that the original name might derive from an old Irish term for remains
or enshrined bones. His theory, by no means implausible, was that
from here Colum Cille's relics were first taken on board a curragh for
Kells.

It was certainly a spot closely linked with reverence for the dead. Mr
MacMillan also mentioned, as had Henry D. Graham writing in 1848,
that local people too, bringing remains of a relative back by sea, would
tend to use this traditional landing-place rather than the jetty in the
neighbouring bay of Port Rònain.

Two 'Iona Boat Songs' are in current circulation, both linked with
the image of a funeral party being rowed along but neither of ancient

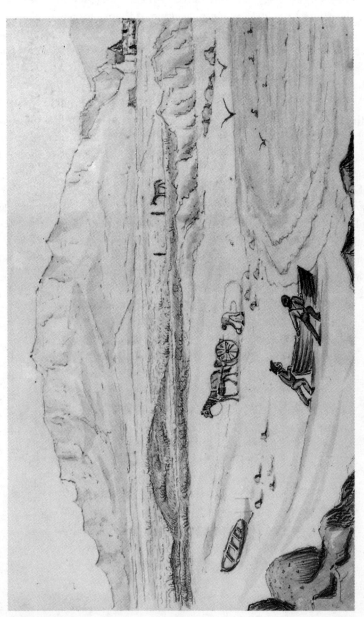

Figure 1. Port nam Mairtear – Martyrs Bay – sketched by visitor Henry D. Graham, *c.*1848–52. The grassy knoll called the Ealadh, where coffins were rested, is clearly seen at the head of the bay. A corner of the nunnery, with the schoolhouse behind is in the top right corner. Photograph courtesy of the RCAHMS.

pedigree. Occasionally, by some stretch of the imagination, they are even attributed to Columban monks. One of them, 'Iomair o, 'illean mhara' is a modern fabrication, made up of words by Kenneth MacLeod and a traditional tune adapted by Marjorie Kennedy Fraser. The Gaelic version of the other – 'Caol Muile' – has in fact nothing to do with Iona but is a nineteenth-century poem in praise of the Sound of Mull by the Revd Dr John MacLeod of Morvern. English words to the same air describe a boat carrying a 'king who to resting is come' and which 'softly glides along … to the dear Isle Iona our home'. This idyllic picture, unruffled by stormy seas, is a twentieth-century composition.

The tune, however, is undoubtedly old and not unlike the type which would have been suited to the chanting of a Gaelic prayer. And 'iorrams' or rowing songs do form part of a recognised body of rhythmic music, sung by the Gaels to accompany work. It is not hard to imagine an iorram resounding to the beat of the oars, as Maclean or MacDonald men rowed the body of their chief towards the Sound of Iona.

Part Two

*An àite guth manaich bidh
geum bà*
*In the place of monks' voices
will be lowing of cattle*

4

Voices of Monks

Before the turn of the first millennium, the focus of religious authority and royal attention had begun to shift inexorably eastward. Dunkeld and Scone grew in status, as did St Andrews – where Constantine II was buried in 952 having retired there as a monk a few years earlier. If Donald Bane's bones were indeed taken to Iona soon after 1097, then he was the last of the Scottish kings to be given that honour. With the deaths of his brother Malcolm Canmore and consort Margaret in 1093 there had already begun the tradition of royal burial in Dunfermline Abbey – which the Queen had founded as the first Benedictine monastery in Scotland.

Neither Viking ravages nor this waning of its political star appear to have finished off religious life on Iona entirely. A community of monks, albeit perhaps much smaller than before, continued to live there and to maintain links southward to Ireland. The names of abbots of Iona appear in the *Annals of Ulster* up until 1099. The devout Queen Margaret, no less, from whose reign stemmed the Continental influences that later crept into the Church on the other side of the country, is credited with helping to keep the Celtic flame kindled on its native hearth. 'Among the other good things which the noble lady did', wrote the chronicler, was to rebuild the Columban monastery of Iona and provide monks with 'fitting revenues for the work of the Lord'.

These statements come from one source alone, the Anglo-Norman Orderic Vitalis who was at school in Normandy during the last years of

Margaret's life. No extant Irish annals make mention of any generosity on her part towards Iona. If the monastic community there was important enough for the Queen to endow, it is at least possible that she would have made a pilgrimage to it, but no records, nor place-names along the route, hint at such a journey. Would she not also have wished to place Benedictine monks on the island as she had begun to do in the east, a step which her son David was to build upon considerably? And for that not to have provoked a reaction from Ireland would have been surprising, as subsequent events were to show.

The reference comes in a passage extolling the piety and good works of Malcolm and Margaret, written during the reign of Henry I of England who was married to their daughter Matilda. One cannot help wondering if Vitalis was simply embellishing Margaret's reputation, by linking her to a place of historic sanctity, for the benefit of Henry and his Queen. Yet this single source has been very seldom questioned, although it is frequently cited in writings on Iona.

There again, famous names have a habit of becoming attached to the Sacred Isle. Margaret's father-in-law, Duncan, and his successor Macbeth are prime examples of this. Centuries later, visitors' curiosity about the highly speculative burial places of these two characters, firmly yoked together thanks to the literary licence of William Shakespeare, was to outstrip even that about where St Columba himself might have ended his days.

Whether the monastic community on Iona did or did not benefit from royal support during the reign of Malcolm and Margaret, its members were soon to come under the wing of a new power to dominate the west coast waterways – a power whose leaders were to approach the status of kings among islesmen. The founder of this MacDonald dynasty, to become known as the Lords of the Isles, was Somerled, who claimed both Norse and Gaelic lineage. The first record of his interest in Iona comes from the *Annals of Ulster* for 1164 when, apparently on Somerled's advice, priests and monks from the island went to Derry which by then had inherited from Kells the headship of the Columban monastic family in Ireland. The delegation's task was 'to meet Colum Cille's successor Flaithbertach Ua-Brolchain' and ask him to take over the abbacy of Iona. Perhaps this was an attempt to regain influence for Iona by strengthening the old links across the Irish Channel, but in any event it was unsuccessful.

To Somerled's son Reginald, however, is attributed first patronage of the Benedictine monastery which was to reinvigorate religious life on Iona for a further three centuries at least. A papal bull dated 9 December 1203 was addressed to the first abbot, Cellach, and assured the new monastery of the Holy See's direct protection. However, this lurch towards Rome proved too alarmingly new for the Irish clergy. In 1204 a high-powered posse of bishops, abbots and Derry monks set sail for Iona and there, if the annals are to be believed, literally cast down the walls of the recently erected church which, in their view, had been built 'in violation of the rights of the community of Iona'. This time, the Abbot of Derry was installed with alacrity in Cellach's place.

No more is heard of this curious *coup*, however, and it has to be assumed that it was not long until Cellach and his Benedictines were reinstated and continued their task of physical and spiritual rebuilding. There were elements of continuity with the old order nevertheless. The abbey complex stood within the same vallum that had sheltered the first wattle cells, and its walls rose up very close to at least three Early Christian high crosses – whose inspiration and significance can hardly have been lost on succeeding generations. Although the Order was of foreign origin, it is probable that the abbots and brethren came mostly from the Gaelic–Norse culture of the Isles; by the fourteenth century that was certainly the case. Most important of all was the fact that the monastery's seal designated it 'of St Columba' and that remained, officially, its name.

The church was considerably expanded and altered from its first simple cruciform shape. Both it and the adjoining monastic buildings were to be restored in different stages in modern times. This recreation, although not true in every detail, does let us more readily imagine the medieval brothers going about their daily round. We see them processing from the cloisters through the nave towards the altar – for the celebration of mass – and, in the hours of darkness, filing silently down the night stair to the choir. The line of black-robed figures will have stood out starkly against the inside walls, white with lime-wash and perhaps resplendent with biblical decoration as so many medieval abbeys were. Every week the brothers chanted the psalter in its entirety and then began again. Thus, observation of the seven offices, day and night, imposed its own rigorous rhythm and the church was central to their lives.

In the chapter-house, matters of discipline and secular concern were dealt with, a chapter from St Benedict's Rule being read before business began. The monks ate together in the refectory, not conversing but listening to the lector reading spiritual texts from his nook a few steps above their heads. There were the bakehouse and brewhouse to run, the sick to be tended in the infirmary and guests to be received. Perhaps it was a visitor, mindful to provide his own secular entertainment, who dropped two medieval playing pieces unearthed centuries later. Made of whalebone, they are delicately carved, one with a simple lattice design and the other depicting a tiny mermaid with a crown on her head and a fish grasped in her hand.

To the inhabitants of Iona the Benedictine monastery was long known simply as 'An Eaglais Mhòr', Gaelic for the big church. Shortly after its establishment, there followed what came to be called 'An Eaglais Dhubh', the black church. Canonesses wearing the habit of the Augustinian order now took their place in the island's unfolding story. It may be that the foundation started out as Benedictine. The *Book of Clanranald* praises Reginald for erecting three monasteries: one of Black Monks in Iona, 'in honour of God and Columba', one of Black Nuns in the same place, and a house of Grey Friars at Saddell in Kintyre. Reginald's sister Beathag is described as a religious woman and 'na cailligh dhuibh' or 'a Black Nun'. She was the Iona Nunnery's first prioress.

The Royal Commission on the Ancient and Historical Monuments of Scotland, whose Iona volume in their Argyll series provides a wealth of information on the island's entire store of ecclesiastical remains, regards the nunnery as one of the best-preserved examples of its kind in the British Isles. It is small and serene, the former living areas and the chapel now green and airy spaces hugged by walls full of rosy-pink granite. But tantalisingly little has come down to us of who exactly walked, sat and prayed within those walls, where they came from and how they kept body and soul together amid their beautiful, but spartan, surroundings.

During repair work in the 1920s workmen discovered, wrapped up and tucked beneath a floor slab, three finely crafted silver gilt spoons and a gold fillet, a delicate hair ornament. At the same period a gold ring and another fillet were found below the floor of the nearby medieval parish church of St Ronan. The spoons are similar to the Coronation anointing spoon but, save for their location, there was nothing to prove that they had a religious rather than a domestic purpose. Were they, perhaps, personal items surrendered by a woman of aristocratic background when she entered the convent? A more prosaic alternative was that they were stolen loot, buried in the ruins for safety and never reclaimed. They can be seen in the National Museum of Scotland but leave us none the wiser as to whether theirs was a dramatic or an ordinary story.

The nunnery was dedicated to St Mary the Virgin. It has been suggested that canonesses from Ireland, where Augustinian houses were common, may have come in to provide the initial training for novices. No doubt unmarried daughters of West Highland families also found their way there, or were sent to enter the convent in due course. Finnguala and Mariota MacInolly, remembered simply on their grave-slab as 'sometime nuns of Iona', were perhaps two such sisters, together in life and in death. On another slab, frozen in stone relief, are the forms of four women, two in lay dress and two in habits and all with their hands devoutly clasped. They gaze out in anonymity. All that may be read of the inscription today are the words '*Hic iacent* ... Here lie ...'.

A plain stone, with no inscription, in a corner of the churchyard used to be pointed out in the nineteenth century as the forlorn marker to a nun who had been obliged to leave holy orders. Henry D. Graham sent a drawing of it to his father, with the note: 'Tombstone of the frail nun ... though it is broken like her vows and cracked like her expectation, poor thing.'

A little more is known about Prioress Anna Maclean who died in 1543 and whose fine memorial tablet was admired and described by several early travellers. She was the daughter of a Donald Maclean, from the same Kingairloch family who supplied two Bishops of the Isles at Iona, Farquhar and Roderick Maclean, in the early sixteenth century. The stone includes charming and symbolic details, such as angels at her pillow and faithful lap-dogs by her side, but of more

practical interest is the clear depiction of her dress. Below the dark
outer robe and over an ankle-length cassock she wears a rochet, the
white pleated surplice which denoted the Augustinian order.

Long-sleeved overgarments of white linen raise the spectre of a
considerable burden of laundry work, for some of the sisters or their
servants at any rate. Servants they will certainly have had. The nuns did
at various stages hold endowments of land in other parts of the
Hebrides, notably Gribun in Mull and the island of Inchkenneth, but
they were also granted the area south of Loch Staonaig on Iona itself.
It is marked off to this day by the low, mossy humps of the Gàradh
Dubh, literally the black wall or enclosure but presumably implying
the wall of the black-robed ones. Here herds will have tended the
nunnery cattle. Perhaps they brought them in from the hills for milking at Buaile nan Cailleach, the fold of the old women – or of the nuns
as the word 'cailleach' can also mean nun, literally 'one who takes
the veil'. This spot lies just on the northern approach to the Staonaig
lands.

The proximity of a nunnery to a monastery inevitably prompted the
occasional ribald speculation by visitors and writers. The most lurid
appears to have circulated on the island itself, according to guide
Angus Lamont in 1848: 'It has been and still is reported that a fellow of
the name of Macruslinn, Russell, disguised in female attire found his
way to this convent and left sixteen of the real sisters in the family way.'

However irreverent such tales, and however wildly exaggerated they
may have become, they did contain a germ of truth. For moral and
financial corruption in religious foundations, at the hands of those who
held spiritual authority over them, was rife in late medieval Scotland.
A stream of complaints to the supreme authority in Rome testified to
the scale of the problem. Iona's particular troubles stemmed from the
lengthy involvement of a major Mull family, the MacKinnons, in the
running of the monastery. There is a heavy hint that the first of
them, Finguine MacKinnon, had inveigled his way into the abbacy by
1359. Earning later notoriety as 'the green abbot', he stood accused of
squandering abbey income on concubines and their offspring, neglect-
ing the fabric of the monastery and granting property and positions of
power to members of his own family.

The task of repairing some of this damage fell in time to Abbot

Dominic MacKenzie who succeeded in 1421. The appearance of this entirely new figure on to the scene, from well outwith the MacKinnon ambit, may have been due to the favourable influence of Donald of Islay, Lord of the Isles. This is speculated by Alan Macquarrie whose useful booklet *Iona through the Ages* traces in detail the labyrinthian turns and twists of the island's monastic life throughout the fifteenth and sixteenth centuries. Iona had remained under the lordship's patronage and a wary concern for its affairs was not unexpected from that quarter. In December 1421 Donald asked the Pope that three vicarages, in Tiree and Mull, be united to Iona as a means of boosting the abbey's revenues.

That supplication, along with the request one month earlier for ratification of Abbot MacKenzie's election, was in all probability carried on the long journey to Rome by an ordinary monk of the community whose Latin name was Dominicus Dominici. Why he was selected for the task of messenger we cannot know, nor whether he wanted to go. The roads and rivers of Europe at that time were alive with people heading for the Holy City, an exciting adventure for a young man from a Hebridean island. On the other hand, the way was hard and hazardous. Dominic had to travel to the south of England, cross the Channel and then find his way through Burgundy, maybe resting at one of the monasteries along the route. From there he had either to toil through the high, snowy mountain passes of the Alps or continue to Provence and the Mediterranean coast, risking attack by pirates on the final sail to Italy.

This duty laid upon him, however, did provide Dominic with a chance to further his own interests and those of his family. And his few paragraphs, set out on parchment and preserved in the Vatican, speak to us down the centuries, giving a fleeting but direct insight into life on Iona under the recent misrule of the MacKinnons.

Dominic's plea was that the Pope grant him dispensation to be the vicar of a parish church, from which he would thus gain the teinds or income. His grounds for this were that the monastery alone could not provide a sufficient living on account of its impoverished and dilapidated state. He declared that 'the timber work and walls of the choir, bell-tower and other surrounding buildings ... are utterly fallen to the ground' and bewailed the fact that part of its lands 'are preyed upon and devastated by wicked and perverse nobles'. Moreover, although hospitality was an important part of the Benedictine Rule, the scale of it seems to have become a burden and the monks themselves 'scarcely have bread, barley or ale' on this account.

More than six weeks at least after his arrival at the *curia*, the papal court where supplications were received, Dominic had received his dispensation but pressed his case further. Arguing again that Iona was too poor to hold out much prospect of a better income, he wanted to be allowed to seek a parish anywhere, whether belonging to the island monastery or not. By this time he was getting weary. He pointed out that he had come from distant parts, 'not without great labours, dangers and expense', and had now spent nearly all his money.

It does appear that he carried out a final task in Rome, however. A few weeks later, in January 1422, a plea was lodged on behalf of Cristina Dominici, nun of 'the monastery of St Mary of Iona', to the effect that she be permitted to hold offices within her order. She was almost certainly Dominic's sister and her request, too, was for ecclesiastical promotion.

Both Dominic and Cristina declared themselves to have 'defect of birth', as the son and daughter of a priest and an unmarried woman. This was not in itself a major obstacle. In the introduction to her second volume of the *Calender of Scottish Supplications to Rome*, editor Dr Annie Dunlop noted that a large proportion of the clergy dispensed as sons of priests came from areas where the Celtic church had once been strong. She suggested that the stricter Roman attitudes to celibacy may not yet have taken firm root.

The mother of priest Dominic's children was probably a local woman. In one of his letters, Dominic the son mentioned 'the religious and other indwellers' of Iona and it is clear that by his day a secular population was well established on the island. Papal records from 1372, referring to the appointment of a rector, had already implied the existence of a parish congregation. And architectural evidence for Teampull Rònain, the medieval parish church, indicates a date from the late twelfth or early thirteenth century.

This simple church is dedicated to St Ronan about whom little is known, but the bay by the present jetty also bears his name. There was an eighth-century abbot called Ronan at Kingarth in Bute and a number of dedications to him exist, on the mainland and in islands named Rona, one off Skye and another north-east of Lewis. The Iona site, however, has only lately taken on fresh significance. Excavations in 1992 revealed that the medieval building stands on the foundations of an earlier one below which, in turn, lie traces of nine dug graves. Remains from these are too slight to determine gender or accurate date but the possibility that these burials could go back as far as the sixth century has not been ruled out by the archaeologists. The graves clearly were in place before the newly discovered rectangular structure was erected over them and this has been tentatively dated at any time between the eighth and twelfth centuries. Given that the parish church then reused the same site, the older building was very probably also a church, its walls of undressed stones held together by clay and plastered with lime-mortar.

The dig brought to light, too, over fifty further grave sites of later date, within and just outside St Ronan's Church. Examination of bone samples has led to the conclusion that here was a cemetery for women, infants and young children. This confirms information consistently recorded by travellers from the late seventeenth century onward that, since medieval times, the women of the island were buried within the nunnery precincts. In 1795 the local minister, the Revd Dugald Campbell, was to note in the first *Statistical Account*: 'Till within these few years all the females were buried at the Nunnery and all the males at the abbey. With few exceptions it is still the case; such is the force of custom and prejudice.'

It may not have been simply the existence of a nunnery that led the local population to bury their womenfolk near to where their sisters in orders lay. The separate burial of women, and separate churches associated with women and with their own graveyard are well documented in early medieval Ireland. Nearer home, a site near St Blane's Chapel in Bute was customarily held to be both a convent and a female cemetery.

Allusion has already been made, when referring to Cladh nan Druinneach in Chapter 1, to the custom of different cemeteries for different purposes. By the nineteenth century, Reeves noted seven burial sites of some kind on Iona, knowledge of which tradition the author has been able to trace to the present day. When the electricity cable was being laid across to Iona in the 1950s, the sandy soil at the head of Port nam Mairtear, near the mound called the Ealadh, was found to contain dozens of human bones. The majority were of adult females. Was this just possibly a special site even earlier than that in the nunnery grounds? Another graveyard discussed earlier (see Chap. 2), Cladh an Diseirt, may include a small chapel not unlike that at St Ronan's. And there is the mysterious Cladh na Meirghe, supposedly a burial place for unbaptised children and which, by accident or design, lies at the head of Gleann an Teampuill – the glen of the temple.

Were there thus several outlying sites for praise or contemplation or for commemorating the dead, at various stages in Iona's monastic history? Whether they were monks or lay people who gathered in the small white church in the lee of Cnoc Mòr, its significance was confirmed by the continuance of worship on that spot. And at some stage, possibly before the nunnery was built but certainly thereafter, it came to be a special place for the women and children of the island. There they were laid to rest, unnamed, their simple shrouds fastened by a bone or brass pin, perhaps of the type also found nearby, and with a handful of white quartz pebbles left gleaming in the earth that covered them.

Throughout the life of the Benedictine monastery the island's population must have grown and the seaways to and from it kept busy. At various times the monks held estates as far south as Kintyre and Islay and as far north as Canna, Skye and North Uist, in addition to many holdings in Mull. Rents had to be collected and no doubt visits made by or to the lay bailies who administered these lands.

There will have been exchanges, too, between the schools of monumental carving that flourished in the fourteenth and fifteenth centuries, on Iona itself as well as on Oronsay and in Kintyre and mainland Lorne. Craftsmen worked at the richly decorated memorials and trained the next generation in their art. From the east shore of Loch Sween in Knapdale, near Doide, the grey chlorite schist which the masons quarried in slabs had to be transported in barges, or on large rafts, up the Argyllshire coast. From Carsaig, round the south coast of Mull, they had to bring sandstone; and from Eilean nam Ban and the Ross of Mull coast blocks of red granite, for general masonry work.

During Abbot MacKenzie's time and just after, in the mid-fifteenth century, major rebuilding was carried out on the abbey church and surrounds. Irish links were again clear, in architectural parallels and in personal contacts. One gravestone bears the legend: 'and Mael-Sechlainn O Cuinn, mason, fashioned it'. Master-mason for the church may have been Donald O Brolchán, who left his name carved on a choir capital. The Irish family of that name had been closely associated with the monastery at Derry and members of it appear to have settled in the West Highlands by the early Middle Ages. Donald may have stayed on in Iona and possibly had descendants. A William and John O Brolchán lived there in 1716 but then disappeared from view.

Pilgrims will again have made their way to Iona, particularly on the great feast days. They may have paused on the path from the shore to pray in St Mary's Chapel, of which only a fragment now stands. They washed their feet in the granite trough at the church's west door before thronging the nave to hear, through a screen, the sacrament celebrated or to touch the monastery's sacred relics. The *Book of Clanranald* records that Donald, Lord of the Isles who died in 1421 donated 'a covering of gold and silver for the relic of the hand of Columba'. This implies that at least one of the saint's precious bones had been brought back at some point, since they were all reputedly taken for safekeeping to Kells and Dunkeld in 849. Relics were vital to attract pilgrims, whose offerings brought income and who were thus positively encouraged. A papal petition from 1428, for example, asks that the faithful visiting the church on Iona on feast days be granted 'three years and as many quarantines of indulgences, to endure in perpetuity'.

Retinues of the noble dead being brought for burial in the Reilig Odhráin had to be received, and the services conducted with due ceremony. Scholars of the period place the small building there, St Oran's Chapel, sometime in the twelfth century and some suggest that it may have been built by the MacDonalds as a family tomb. It is traditionally the burial place of Angus Og MacDonald and of both his son John and grandson Donald, who were first and second Lords of the Isles. The hereditary bards and historians who compiled the *Book of*

Clanranald paint a suitably regal picture in their description of John's
funeral: 'The abbots and monks and vicars came to meet him, as it was
the custom to meet the King of the Hebrides and his services and
waking were honourably performed during eight days and eight nights
and he was laid in the same grave with his father in the Church of
Odhran in the year of our Lord 1380.'

In the museum behind Iona Cathedral they convey power yet, these
men: Colum son of Ruari MacLeod, his galley waiting with furled sail;
or Gilbride son of Finguine, shield and sword at the ready. Others stare
impassively above the visitors' heads, hounds at their feet. In the flesh
they must truly have been formidable. But internal discord began to
enmesh the lordship and its fortunes declined as the fifteenth century
drew to a close. With the final forfeiture of its possessions in 1493, Iona
lost both a benefactor and a protected place within the heart of
medieval Gaeldom.

From 1499, following a papal decree, the Bishop of the Isles and the
Abbot of Iona were one and the same. The Bishopric of Sodor, the
diocese encompassing all the west coast islands – which to Norse rulers
had been the *Sudreyar* or southern isles – was earlier based in the Isle
of Man. After the acquisition of Man by the English in 1387 the
Bishopric of the Isles appears to have been centred for a period on
Snizort in Skye, although the details are obscure. It is equally unclear
whether Iona's monks were officially formed into a diocesan chapter,
thus to endow their abbey with the full status of a cathedral. It is clear,
however, that in 1499 John Campbell, Bishop of the Isles, also became
commendator of Iona – that is to say he had titular right to its benefices
or income – and that the abbey church operated *de facto* as the
Cathedral of the Isles.

Just north-east of the cathedral buildings stand remains of the inside
wall of Tigh an Easbuig or the Bishop's House, probably built sometime in the sixteenth century for the holders of the office. Whether any
of them used it as a principal residence is not certain but they will have
lived there while visiting the island to attend to business. Succession as
bishop-cum-commendator swung mainly between various branches of
the Campbell and Maclean families and there is an impression that
control over the properties and revenues was of keener concern to
some of these men than strong spiritual leadership. Portions of Iona's

lands began to be feued off. Prior Alan Maclean and five monks signed one of these land grants in 1532, but this is not necessarily a sign of the small size of the community. Abbey charters of the time generally included only a short list of names. It is likely, however, that by this time their numbers were declining.

> An I mo chridhe, I mo ghràidh
> An àite guth manaich bidh geum bà
> Ach mun tig an saoghal gu crìch
> Bidh I mar a bha.

> In Iona of my heart, Iona of my love
> In the place of monks' voices will be lowing of cattle
> But ere the world shall come to an end
> Iona shall be as it was.

This saying has appeared in print from at least the late eighteenth century. When it began to circulate in the oral tradition is impossible to tell, nor when it came to be attributed to St Columba. It is not one of his prophecies, as recorded by Adomnán at least. The lines convey a sentiment which later generations, perhaps, felt he might well have expressed. Yet it is just as credible that they were composed and first spoken in the middle of the sixteenth century, by a Benedictine brother who sensed the winds of change. The sound of monks chanting their cycle of psalms, day in and day out, would soon be heard no more. It was the end of an epoch that had lasted almost exactly one thousand years.

5

Lowing of Cattle

The last bishop-commendator of Iona before the Reformation, Alexander Gordon, and the bishop-elect in 1560, John Campbell of Cawdor, both sympathised with the moves towards Protestantism afoot within the Church for some time and it may be assumed that the reformed faith was adopted without undue upheaval on the island. There is no evidence to the contrary. Documentary references from the later sixteenth century imply that the dwindling remnant of monks and nuns on Iona simply stayed on in their buildings for a few decades. Some may have been absorbed into the ranks of new clergy, others will eventually have left or died.

A story persists that Uamh nan Cailleach, 'the Nuns' Cave' on a wild stretch of coast near Carsaig in Mull, is so called because Iona's nuns fled there at the Reformation but this is probably a romanticised tale. The interior does have numerous inscribed crosses, but many of them are thought to date from a much earlier period, as do similar carvings in another cave farther west at Scoor. It may have provided secluded refuge, by accident or by choice, for one or more nuns at some point; or the association with Iona may simply derive from its likely use as a shelter by the masons quarrying freestone there for the medieval buildings. In any event, Prioress Marion Maclean was reconfirmed by the crown as recipient of nunnery revenues in 1567 and not until 1574 did she finally give up the lands, with the consent of her convent, in favour of Hector Maclean of Duart.

The previous year two monks at least had still been resident, 'James

M'Clayne' and 'Murchardus', who put their names to a land grant document. Some of the last members of the community may have taken away, perhaps to the Continent, what remained of the monastery's books and manuscripts. The fate of Iona's library has never been certain. What there was during Columban times probably fell victim to Viking attack or was lost track of after removal to Ireland. In 1953 there was an archaeological expedition from St Andrews University to Cairnburg Mòr, one of the Treshnish Islands, following up a tradition that the library had been hidden there. But the soil yielded no answer to the mystery.

The Presbyterian structure which we know in the Church of Scotland today did not of course arise overnight, nor were the offices of the old system swept away all at once. Soon after the Reformation parliament met in 1560, superintendents, initially five, were appointed to oversee a new scheme of districts. John Carswell was made superintendent of Argyll and five years later he was also presented to the Bishopric of the Isles, which was still centred on Iona and to which was still attached the office of commendator.

Carswell, whose permanent home was at Carnasserie Castle on mainland Lorne, is remembered particularly as translator of the *Book of Common Order*. This was the first book to be printed in Gaelic, in 1567, albeit in the classical language of the bards rather than in the daily tongue of the people. Tradition in Argyll recalls him rather unkindly, harsh in the exaction of church dues and in his zeal for the reformed cause. But his influence along with that of the Campbells, firmly Protestant and steadily expanding their territory in Argyll, must have helped ensure that the new Church took root in the area from an early stage.

Information about how the spiritual needs of the local population were met in the immediate post-Reformation era is patchy. Whether the last parish priest to say mass in Teampull Rònain fled or converted we do not know. But by 1573 a Fingon MacMillan, dean of Mull was minister of Iona. The task of the Church to find clergy of the reformed faith for every parish in the land was daunting but even the scattered corners of the Highlands and Islands were by no means totally overlooked. The energy of Bishop Carswell, who had also taken on responsibility for paying the stipends of ministers in his diocese, may well have helped in Iona's case. And there was some continuity in the bishopric with the succession in 1573 of John Campbell, the same man who had held it briefly around 1560. He seems to have spent some time on Iona, particularly towards the end of his life. He was resident there in 1585, when he made a will, and he died there a few years later.

From the *Fasti*, the record of Church of Scotland clergy, we find Hew Maclean listed for Iona from 1630 but his ministry may only have lasted about a decade. The Synod of Argyll, created in 1638, records in its minutes for May 1642 – when it had met in Iona – a mention of his widow, Finguel MacAllan. And the next year it considered that 'the long vacancy of the kirk of Icollumkill' would be 'prejudicial' to the state of the Church there. In other words, it appeared to be well aware that buildings had to be used, if they were not to collapse, and that a possibly errant flock needed regular pastoral care.

The synod members agreed to transfer Martin McIlvra from Kilfinichen and Kilviceuen in Mull to Iona in 1643. Moreover, they had arranged for John McLachlan, of the smaller parish of Seil in the Firth of Lorne, to fill in at Iona just prior to that. At their meetings in 1656, one of which was again held on Iona, the Synod expressed concern about money allotted to keeping up the fabric of the church there. They also noted the suggestion that a school be set up on Iona; that Daniell Maclean, tutor to Duart, was willing to contribute to its maintenance; and that they themselves would try to find a qualified young man as schoolmaster. By the next year, however, Maclean had not fulfilled a promise to attend to repairs of the Bishop's House, possibly intended as the school, and no more was heard of the proposal.

Meanwhile, the Revd Martin McIlvra had incurred the Synod's displeasure and it had deposed him in 1648. The grounds were that in 1645 he had associated with Sir Lachlan Maclean of Duart, who had been excommunicated for supporting the royalist cause in the first phase of the Civil War, and had preached twice to him, on one occasion in Iona. Ripples of dramatic events on the national stage were thus spreading outward to every corner, as the relationship of Church and State jolted forward in fragmented and confusing stages throughout the seventeenth century.

It is more than a hundred years after the Reformation that there is an impression of real neglect. The seven medieval parishes of Mull appear to have been treated at first as one large parish until, early in the seventeenth century, they were regrouped into three. The parish in which Iona lay was Kilfinichen and Kilviceuen. This still covered a big area and the minister lived on the Mull side of the water. By the 1760s visitors were reporting that he crossed to Iona only four times a year to take services and this will presumably have been the case since the departure of Mr McIlvra. Visitors remarked too on the decline of the once great centre of faith and fame. Only one seventeenth-century burial of a significant figure has been recorded. Dr John Beaton, known as An t-Ollamh Muileach and a member of the renowned Mull family of physicians, died in 1657. In 1674 Donald Beaton laid an inscribed, signed slab on his kinsman's grave in the Reilig Odhráin. By 1688 the St Oran's Chapel was described by Sacheverell as 'a decayed oratory'. Tigh an Easbuig, which had served as official residence for the Bishops of the Isles for well over a century, was roofless and the abbey church was ruinous. A hundred years later Pennant found the floor of the nunnery church 'covered some feet thick with cow-dung'. The cattle had for some time been lowing within the ancient walls.

Where there were cattle, however, there were people. The earliest surviving estate map for Iona is dated 1769, but the pattern of land use it carefully recorded matches any earlier written descriptions. There is no logical reason why the general layout will have changed substantially since the medieval period or even before.

The maker of the map, William Douglas, marked out the arable and hill land with comments such as 'sandy soil with a mixture of black earth' or 'green pasture with a mixture of meadow'. Along the island's eastern edge and right around the northern shore to Calva; across its central belt and over a broad swathe of the present Machair; from Ceann na Creige to beyond Dùn Bhuirg, Douglas indicates land under cultivation. Some of this will have been worked too during both the earlier periods of monastic settlement. Adomnán tells us that the Columban monks tilled the soil of 'the western plain'. More may have been put under the cas-chrom or foot plough as the population grew. On sheltered slopes and crannies all over the island are patches of rig-marks, now smooth and green, silent testimony to the toil of former generations.

From the late seventeenth century travel accounts remarked on the fertility of the island, its good crops and grazing and Sacheverell saw 'great herds of cows feeding'. As elsewhere in the Highlands, cattle were by then the mainstay of the economy, adding a stronger commercial element to the basic, year-by-year subsistence. They did provide food and part of the rental in kind, for example the two stones of cheese and two quarts of butter due to Maclean of Duart in 1679. But they also brought in cash income from their sale; the Iona tenants had to pay £190 to Maclean that same year.

In the autumn the men and boys must have ferried the beasts bound for lowland trysts over the Sound of Iona, or possibly swum them across as they certainly did their horses, to walk them through Mull. They would meet up with the droves coming down from the north, or in from Tiree and Coll, the jostling black lines all tramping towards Achnacraig and the ferries to Kerrera and the mainland. The parish minister for Torosay wrote in 1792 that 2,000 beasts went by this route annually.

Each August there was, too, the great Mull horse fair. Riding through Mull in 1760 Pococke noted that the horses were small and hardy and that some three hundred, at £4 apiece, were exported from the island most years. The Iona folk certainly bred horses and they may well have been going to the Mull fair from its earliest days. Cattle were sold there too, in May and October, and the event – 'the most considerable fair in the West Highlands' according to Ramsay of Ochtertyre in the late eighteenth century – was thought to have been established for many generations by then. These must have been tremendous occasions, with dealers, drovers, pedlars and hundreds of local folk swarming around the booths and pens that spilled down the hillside at Druim-Tigh-Mhic-Ghille-Chatain in Glen Aros, over several days of bargaining and carousing. Later, by the end of the nineteenth century, the fair, now mostly for horses, had abandoned the site with the picturesque name – the ridge of the house of the son of Gille Chatain – and moved to Salen.

Out across Iona's hills those who tended the stock have left occasional clues as to how the land was used, some easier to interpret than others. Place-names including 'buaile' dot the landscape. These were often spots where cattle might be brought together for the women and girls to milk them. The hillocks and gullies of the island's north-west are neatly divided up by a network of grey stone walls, in some ancient form of apportionment reaching back well before the crofting era. In the former nunnery lands south of the loch lies Gàradh Eachain Oig, the enclosure of young Hector who was said to be of the Duart Macleans. The boundaries that can just be picked out through the heather, the rig-marks and the foundations of buildings nearby, may thus date from the seventeenth or even the sixteenth century.

By the time places came to be mapped in print in any detail, in the mid-nineteenth century, a spot at the very south of the island was already known as Port Làraichean, the bay of the ruins. The dwelling perched on the raised beach above the bay, with its circular enclosure against the cliff, must have been occupied at one time (perhaps by herds for the cattle), but its name implies that it had been long abandoned. Just where the hills rise south of the central plain the people made a cairn, Carn Leth an Rathaid, which literally means half-road cairn. It was mid-way between those farthest signs of human activity and the village where most of the people lived.

'A considerable citie was in the Isle of old' wrote Robert Sibbald for *MacFarlane's Geographical Collections* of 1693. The main settlement was known as the Baile Mòr or 'big village'. These may seem to be slight exaggerations but when all the houses were concentrated together, in the shadow of tall walls and steeples, the effect may have been quite impressive, particularly when viewed from the sea. As Pennant's party sailed away, he found that 'the view of Iona, its clustered town, the great ruins and the fertility of the ground' contrasted pleasantly with the bare rocks of Mull ahead.

The old main street, of large granite cobbles, linked the south-east corner of the cathedral complex and Maclean's Cross. Here three paths appeared to converge. One led south towards Port Rònain, one of the main possible landing-places; and another directly to the door of Teampull Rònain, the parish church. The third was Sraid nam Marbh, the old route for carrying coffins from Port nam Mairtear, which curved across the fields and round behind the site of the nunnery before reaching the junction at Maclean's Cross. It is not hard to imagine this as a spot where people would converge too, to exchange news and talk over the business of the township. Their low cottages lay

huddled between the shoreline and the street with a few more
scattered where the later parish church was to be built. Stone with
which to build them was plentiful but many were probably even more
humble, made of turf, wattle and clay, their thatch of straw or heather
bound down with heather rope.

In 1772 Pennant mentioned another road, narrower than the others,
pointing towards the hills. Tracks will have been created wherever
people needed to go and the 1769 map indicates that one did lead to
the Lochan Mòr, by then marked 'moss'. For a few decades after this
area was drained in the mid-eighteenth century, families will have
gathered there in spring to cut peat, carrying it home in late summer
in creels on their backs. But before that they must have had to cross to
Mull for peat, as they did again later, or fall back on driftwood or turf
for fuel.

Pennant also noted a curious feature at the south-east corner of
the cathedral church: 'two parallel walls about twelve feet high and ten
feet distant from each other'. This was said to have formed a covered
corridor from the buildings to the sea, from which he concluded that
the meaning of its name, 'dorus tràigh', was 'the door to the shore'. The
only other published reference to this is in the Revd Archibald
MacMillan's guidebook, written more than a century later. He talks
about 'dorus tràth' – time door – and cites the authority of a native,
long since dead, who had seen them. This was almost certainly Angus
Lamont, whose own manuscript description is intriguing:

> The writer also recollects to have seen, when a boy, part of an arch
> in shape and size of a small bridge, beyond where the public house
> now stands. This the natives called 'dorus tràth' or time door.
> There were four of these doors or ports in the town, through
> which none had access to pass or repass after fixed hours at night
> and day.

Lamont's family came to Iona from Ulva in the late eighteenth
century. The public house to which he refers was the cottage that
served as an inn, at the head of Port Rònain and approximately where
Iona Cottage stands today. The remnant of arch which he claimed to
have seen, therefore, was near to the nunnery precincts. The word
'tràth' can mean time or season but also, more specifically, prayer-time.

So, were the boundaries of the first township, that had begun to form around the Early Christian monastery and which undoubtedly mushroomed in the medieval period, marked off or enclosed in some way by these 'ports'? Was there a curfew? Or could it be that by Lamont's day the notion of 'after fixed hours' had become mingled with vague, recycled memories of days punctuated by the tolling bell, calling monks and nuns in from the fields, perhaps to pass through these arches on their way to divine office?

The relationship between the two settlements, sacred and secular, will of necessity have been a close one in earliest times. The religious houses needed extra help to work the land or provide specialist skills, and in return the locals had, at the very least, a place to build a house. Subsequently they found themselves tenants of, first, the Macleans of Duart and then the Campbells, but not a great deal will have altered in their seasonal round of wresting a livelihood from the soil as best they could.

How strongly or universally, however, did they take up the religious affiliation of their now Protestant landlords? And did no vestiges of their former faith linger, in a place so rich in remains and associations? Any clear-cut answer is elusive, especially as several different influences may have played a part.

In 1625 the Iona people found in their midst Father Patrick Hegarty, member of a mission to the Hebrides and parts of the northwest mainland, from the Irish Franciscan College at Louvain in Belgium. This task was not without hazard, since the priests risked imprisonment if the law caught up with them. In the Ross of Mull Fr Hegarty encountered opposition from Maclean of Duart although one of his converts there was Gillean Maclean, brother of the chief. Fellow priest Cornelius Ward converted Maclaine of Lochbuie the same year and between them they won back over 270 individuals in Mull. Fr Ward's report noted that 'The people of the Hebrides ... have a great devotion to St Columba and venerate him as their patron and apostle.'

In Colum Cille's isle, however, Fr Hegarty made only three converts and then four more on a second visit in 1630. On the earlier occasion he said mass three times, the first such celebration on the island since the Reformation but only those over the age of 70 will have had any clear memory of those days. And we cannot tell how many inhabitants there were in the 1620s, nor assume that they were all, or even most of them descended from the lay population of the 1560s.

Soon after Fr Hegarty's visits, in the mid-1630s, there was new activity in and around the cathedral church. Locals may even have been used for unskilled labouring, as the nave and south choir aisle were blocked off and stonework repaired. These alterations were designed to bring the building back into active service as Cathedral of the Isles, and were part of the ill-fated programme by Charles I to restore to prominence within Church doctrine certain aspects of the liturgy previously set aside. This was to provoke fierce reaction in Scotland. The General Assembly of 1638 abolished episcopacy and Neil Campbell, last Bishop of the Isles at Iona, was deposed. After the Restoration of 1660 the site of the bishopric moved to Rothesay and King Charles's walls in Iona continued to crumble with the rest.

The final abandonment of bishops within the Church of Scotland came at its formal establishment, with royal assent, in 1690. A minority of clergymen did not accept this and their desertion led effectively to the beginnings of the Scottish Episcopal Church. Among them may have been Duncan Bethune, minister of Kilfinichen and Kilviceuen since 1682 but whose entry in the *Fasti* states: 'Though much beloved by his parishioners, he declined to conform to Presbyterianism and left the charge soon after the Revolution'. He had Iona too in his care at this period, presumably visiting it four times a year as his successors are documented to have done. And couples wishing to be married will have crossed the water to go to him. Did his beliefs influence any of these parishioners who held him in such affection?

On the other hand, if the people of Iona had become thoroughly wedded to the Protestant faith by the early seventeenth century, how did they react to the attempted restoration of the cathedral in the 1630s? If they saw this as a tangible sign, on their very doorstep, of the King's interference in the Church's affairs in Scotland, then they might have been expected to turn aside altogether from the building and what it stood for. Yet Sacheverell, in 1688, stated that in the absence of a minister the people 'constantly assemble in the great church on Sundays where they spend most part of their day in private devotion'. And when they came to use English as well as Gaelic, it was as 'the cathedral' that 'an Eaglais Mhòr' was translated, never as 'the abbey'.

It is undoubtedly also true that until the mid-eighteenth century, the locals played a part in the continuing decline of the buildings. They cheerfully quarried them for building material, allowed debris to pile up and cattle to roam unhindered through the precincts. They also regularly reused the carved, medieval tombstones in the Reilig Odhráin, although this could as readily be seen as an action honouring their own kin rather than as a mark of disrespect. Such shreds of evidence as exist are themselves contradictory or they may simply reflect the fact that the people's own affiliation to the historic sites was ambivalent or changed with the generations. Mrs Maclean of Torloisk, visiting in 1814, was critical of the general air of neglect and relayed from her guide, the schoolmaster, a story to the effect that some still alive could remember when the floors of the religious houses were entire 'and dances carried on there with great spirit'.

The Revd Dr John Walker, on the other hand, who was there in 1764, echoes Sacheverell's account of the people gathering in the ruins on a Sunday. His specific addition that they also repair 'to Columba's tomb and to the Chapells of several different Saints' confirms that this spontaneous devotion was focused on the cathedral and not St Ronan's, which had properly been their parish church. As late as 1795 the local minister described the latter as still entire but 'tottering' and it may have fallen into disuse very much earlier. Furthermore, during Martin McIlvra's brief tenure, in the 1640s, it was intended that he use the repaired cathedral church for parish services. If he did so, then this may have been the last place of regular worship for the islanders and so have retained their loyalty.

Part of the commission that led Walker to undertake his tour of the islands was from the Church of Scotland, to report on the state of religion and education. He also observed in Iona that the people had 'many wild and romantic notions concerning religion and invisible things. Though they know not what popery is, the vestiges of it they suck in with their milk, which appear in many of their opinions and practices.' Apart from implying a continued reverence for Columba and other saints by praying in the chapels, he is not specific about signs of Roman Catholicism in the people's worship itself. Rather, he may have been referring to the host of superstitious customs still very much

alive on the island. He mentions one, the carrying of a coffin round
the cathedral before a burial, which he attributed to 'great regard' for
the ancient buildings. The parish minister, however, took a stricter
view and had recently put a stop to the practice. Such echoes of a dim
and distant pagan past may have been tolerated more openly in pre-
Reformation days or they may have revived to some degree during the
years of intermittent ministerial care. Although the persistence of such
customs is corroborated by other travellers' accounts, which became
much more numerous towards the end of the eighteenth century, none
hint that the population was by then other than entirely Presbyterian
in its religious adherence.

Walker considered it unsurprising that the Iona people should be
'remarkable for superstition beyond their neighbours' and felt that
'their unlimited veneration for antiquity' ensured a fund of marvel and
legend. Yet it was noted in earlier chapters that neither general lore
rooted in pre-Christian beliefs nor that surrounding Colum Cille in
particular were exclusive to Iona. Such lore was widespread throughout the Gaidhealtachd. And, as already noted, the local population of
Iona is unlikely to have been of the same stock throughout the entire
time that its venerable institutions evolved.

Who then were the people and where did they come from?
Although lack of documentation makes verification difficult, it is reasonable to assume that a number came into the island in the wake of
the Macleans' gradual assumption of ownership through the late sixteenth and seventeenth centuries. One instance has trickled down
through oral tradition. At the battle of Inverkeithing in 1651, a few
MacInnes men buried the body of Eachainn Ruadh nan Cath, the
Maclean chief. For this they were rewarded with land in Iona.

Red Hector of the Battles was the chief's name but this last bloody
affray had cost his islands dear. It is said that only 40 Macleans came
home out of 800 and that 140 had gone from the Ross of Mull and Iona
alone. Within a generation the Macleans, deeply in debt, were ill-
prepared to resist a long and unequal tussle with the Campbells over
possession of their territory. In the course of this, in 1675, twenty-four
heads of household in Iona were denounced by the Earl of Argyll as
'rebels' for not having already removed themselves 'furth and frae
the lands'. A few were Macleans, but most were listed only by their

patronymics, such as Dougald son of Ronald or Malcolm son of big Finlay.

Whether any of these families did leave or stayed on, none will have escaped the effects of the other major population scourge of the times. Alongside the depredations of constant feuding and war, seasons of lean harvest haunted these centuries. The late 1690s brought a series of severe crop failures everywhere and the malnutrition and sickness that followed resulted in the worst mortality for generations. The minister for the Ross of Mull and Iona was to record in the *Statistical Account* that the famine had nearly depopulated the whole parish. People died upon the roadside and, even a century later, 'King William's days' were still remembered with horror.

No accounts by travellers to Iona have come down to us between that of Dean Monro, who does not mention the local population, in 1549 and that of William Sacheverell in 1688. The latter was informed that eighty families lived on the island although this number probably fell sharply during the dearth of the next decade. But however erratic its population growth and decline may have been, there is no reason to think that there was ever any total break in settlement on the island. Successive cores, perhaps quite small, may have held on through various changes in the island's fortunes. Newcomers from surrounding parts of the Mull estates, or from farther afield, will have integrated quickly, sharing the same language, culture and religion. As the generations passed, all will have strengthened their sense of attachment to the landscape they worked and to the antiquities around them.

An example of how relatively quickly such roots were put down comes from the land itself. The island taken over by the Macleans already had one internal division, the wall at Loch Staonaig marking off the area formerly owned by the nunnery. They kept this, making it together with the north-east corner into a holding for one tenant plus sub-tenants or servants. The remaining heads of household shared the fertile central stretch, working the arable strips allotted to them by turn each year in the old system known as runrig. The system may have been in place while Iona was still church land but, as we have noted, those operating it then are likely to have given way to succeeding waves of incomers. Yet in 1755 the fifteen joint tenants of the West End, requesting the renewal of their lease, argued that they had already possessed the land 'time out of memory'.

The man who gave I Chaluim Chille its name also survived as a strong element in local tradition through to the end of the seventeenth century, when Martin was firmly rebuked for suggesting that the saint may not have been buried there. Moreover, individual claims to a link with Colum Cille were persistent. Both Sacheverell and Martin recorded the strange case of 'Clan vic n' oster' named after the Latin *ostiarii* meaning door-keepers. This family were said to have held this office in the saint's day but once displeased him and he then cursed them. They would never exceed a certain number, eight or five in the different accounts, and the man Martin met was reputedly the very last of the line. In 1773, Boswell and Johnson had as guide a man who termed himself 'descendant of St Columba's cousin'. And even into the 1980s it was possible to hear about a family, the Blacks of Cnoc Cùil Phàil, whose ancestor was held to have come in from Ireland as companion of the saint. Perhaps 'kindred of Colum Cille' was akin to the phrase 'time out of memory' and these were simply ways by which people affirmed links that were strong and old and in some respect meaningful to them.

6

Upon his Own Particular Lot

For much of the period generally termed the Dark Ages, up to 1000 AD, Iona had been a place of central importance in the history of Scotland. Sufficient documentation and references have survived to allow us a fair understanding of the activity both centred in and spawned from the monastery there. By contrast, the two centuries following the very end of monastic settlement were, in a sense, the island's own dark ages. As we have seen, only fragmentary evidence can be pieced together about who lived there and how the land was worked. It is not until the mid-eighteenth century that Iona's local population comes fully into the light, illuminated by estate papers, parish and school records and a cascade of travellers' accounts. From then on their story treads a path similar, in many respects, to that of other communities throughout the Highlands and Islands.

Whoever did live on Iona in the first decade of the seventeenth century, however, witnessed one event that was to have long-lasting resonance among those same communities. This was the assent by nine Gaelic chiefs to the Statutes of Icolmkill. There must have been a bustle around Tigh an Easbuig in August 1609 as Andrew Knox, Bishop of the Isles, arrived to set up a court which included a notary public and seven witnesses. Among the chiefs he had escorted or summonsed there were Maclean of Duart and Maclaine of Lochbuie, both from Mull, along with MacDonald of Dunnyveg in Islay and MacPhie of Colonsay. Several more were from the north – MacDonalds of Sleat and of Clanranald, MacLeod of Harris, MacKinnon of Strath in Skye, and MacQuarrie of Ulva. The galleys bringing the chiefs may have beached on the white sands of Tràigh Bàn nam Manach, before they and their followers struck out over the grassland to join the assembled company.

Nothing quite like this gathering could have been seen on the island since the great funeral parties attending burials of the Lords of the Isles. Angus Lamont recorded the account still current in 1848: 'A great assembly of all the chiefs in the isles ... fixed their tents upon a ridge of gravily land or bank in the lot of Clachanach on the east end of the island, as you pass to the lots occupied by the MacArthurs and the Blacks, and called to this day Iomaire nan Achd, the statute ridge.' This tradition is known yet by local people. The spot runs parallel with the road, on either side of the granite cross erected to the Duchess of Argyll in 1878.

The bond drawn up by Knox was a key component in a strategy already mapped out some years before by James VI and designed to plant 'civilitie' in the lawless and insubordinate corners of his kingdom. Terms included a reduction in military retinues and restriction on firearms, a ban on the harbouring of fugitives and the vagabond bands of poets and minstrels who often ate and drank their hosts' cellars dry, and the reinforcing of adherence to the religion and education of the state. When the chiefs renewed their bond in 1616, this last clause was strengthened. All their children over the age of 9 were to be sent to Lowland schools and none who did not speak and write English were to inherit property or tenant crown lands.

All of this was intended not to subdue the chiefs by force nor to undermine their position, but gradually to alter their manners and attitude and draw them into the landed society of Lowland Scotland. Ultimately, although the period of transition was to be a long one, this is what happened. The breakdown of the once close links between chief and people is often associated in popular imagination with the last Jacobite rebellion of 1745, and its disastrous aftermath, but the beginnings of that change reach much further back.

From the establishment's standpoint, this transition represented a move towards 'civilisation'. The foundations were laid that August day on Iona, a place where piety, learning and artistry had once flourished on a level that was by any standard highly civilised – and thoroughly steeped in Gaelic culture. The irony may not have been intentional. Rather, the island was doubtless chosen because it was the seat of the bishopric and neutral compared to the clan territories of, say, Islay or Mull. Moreover, it may still have commanded respect as a holy place, where an oath sworn could be regarded as sacrosanct.

No chief ever had his stronghold on Iona and it had thus probably escaped the worst consequences of these volatile times, but the people can hardly have been unaware of the feuding and freebooting that did indeed stalk much of the western seaboard. Just around the south-east tip of the Ross of Mull, above the bay called Port Bheathain, the Macleans once fought furiously with the MacPhies of Colonsay. Vivid and bloodthirsty details embellish the story to this day – the Beaton bowmen's skill with the arrow, slicing the heads from the bog cotton as they hurried towards the battle; the nine buckets of MacPhie thumbs collected as their vanquishers hacked at hands on the gunnels of the fleeing boats.

The degree to which Iona was involved directly in the final spasms of warfare that shook the Highlands is unclear. Loyalty to the Macleans is likely to have been maintained for a period after that family lost its ascendancy over the Mull lands to the increasingly powerful House of Argyll. Indeed, even as late as 1773, Dr Johnson reported a lingering allegiance to the Macleans among the people of Iona, although any judgement on that occasion may have been slightly biased by the presence of Sir Alan Maclean of Inchkenneth who accompanied him. We do not know if any Iona men fought with Sir John Maclean in the royalist uprising of 1690, but twenty-five did join the garrison of Cairnburg, in the Treshnish Islands, during the 1715 rebellion. When brought to Duart Castle in April 1716 to deliver up their arms, one Lachlan MacFarlane confessed that the rebels in Cairnburg had made him 'their officer of Icolmkill'.

By the time of the 1745 campaign, the only certain local involvement was that of tacksman John Maclean, who lived on the island from 1738 to 1757 and was probably descended from branches of the family in Coll and north Mull. He piloted a Spanish ship carrying money and arms from Iona to Barra and was imprisoned for three months as a result. The Prince's own wanderings after Culloden never reached as far south as Iona, despite the faint trace of a story to that effect. Mrs

James MacArthur Sligineach, born Catherine MacCormick in 1822, used to say that she once met a man who had seen 'the yellow-haired laddie' sail down the Sound. This belongs fairly clearly to the 'Prince Charlie was here' school of romantic myth, although it is not impossible that it also contains an echo of someone local going off to, or returning from, that ill-fated conflict. The late Donald Morrison from the neighbouring Ross of Mull could still point out the very spot on the peat moss where several young men from the township threw down their spades and set off, whenever news came that the Prince had landed.

Before the 1745 campaign ever began, however, Iona found itself subject to a new policy with regard to land tenure, pioneered by the second Duke of Argyll. Over his Mull and Tiree estates in 1737 he pursued a course, already begun in Kintyre, whereby farm leases or 'tacks' were offered for open auction at a fixed rent rather than automatically allocated on the basis of family or political loyalty. It was an early sign of changes to come, eventually, almost everywhere in the Highlands. Pressure to improve both financial and land management continued under succeeding dukes and in 1770 John, fifth Duke, inherited the Argyll lands at their most extensive, reaching from Kintyre up almost as far as Inverness-shire. His zeal for agricultural reform led to a permanent change in the pattern of landholding on Iona and, as a consequence, to its landscape.

The companion volume to this one relates in detail the measures attempted by the fifth Duke to expand the economy of the island: fishing, kelping, short experiments in flax spinning and marble quarrying. Younger members of the population also augmented the family income through seasonal employment on the mainland, as harvest workers or servants. And a number took up military service, although by now on the side of the establishment. There was an episode in 1799 when, for reasons unexplained, three Iona tenants assaulted the Duke's recruiting officer and were consequently evicted. Only six years earlier there was no hint of reluctance to enlist when the chamberlain brought new soldiers for the Argyllshire Fencibles from the Ross of Mull and Iona to their headquarters at Stirling. In fact, an Iona boy who attached himself to the recruits was fed and clothed and finally accepted; although another, Neil MacArthur, who also followed the party in hope of joining up was not considered fit for service and was paid off.

The fifth Duke ordered a census of his Argyll lands in 1779 and from this we have the earliest firm population figure for Iona, 249 individuals. The numbers climbed steadily in the last decades of the eighteenth century and stood at 384 when another estate list was made in 1804. By this time the Duke was convinced that only a radical move away from the communal, runrig system to individual tenancies would give people the incentive to improve their methods of cultivation and ensure a sound return to the estate. He had therefore instructed his Chamberlain for Mull and Morvern to divide up the farms and encourage 'every man to build his house upon his own particular lot'. On Iona, thirty holdings or crofts were created and the first nine-year leases ran from 1802. Gradually the tenants erected stone boundary walls along their fields and built their new houses. The village was relocated in a single street above the shoreline and occupied by those with a trade, such as weavers, carpenters, shoemakers, fishermen and labourers.

The crofting community of Iona did not come into being due to clearance from fertile glens to make way for more lucrative sheep-walks, as was to be the case in other areas. Nor was it squeezed on to poor and rocky sections of coastline, where additional occupations such as kelp burning were essential for survival. The Iona crofts were made from the good arable land of which each had on average 7–8 acres, plus its share of the hill pasture. The size of these holdings was generous compared to many later created elsewhere, in places such as Lewis or north-west Sutherland. The Chamberlain for Mull and Iona was able to report in 1805 that he had no cause to complain about the ability of the crofters to pay their rents.

The names on the 1779 list plus the register of marriages and baptisms which the minister began in 1804, along with a smattering of family tradition, help us re-create to a degree that first crofting community. Some of the surnames were already well established, indicating one of the strongest lines of continuity in the island's more recent history. In the township to the north of the village, called the East End, there were MacDonalds in Calva and Ardionra, MacKillops at Lagandorain, Blacks at Cnoc Cùil Phàil and MacFarlanes at Boineach (later known as Bishop's Walk). Two MacArthur brothers,

Figure 2   Catherine, wife of weaver Coll MacDonald, filling spools outside Tigh nam Beart, Iona village, 1920s. Photography by courtesy of Pam Finlayson.

Donnachadh Ruadh (red-haired Duncan) and Iain Dubh (dark-haired John), were allocated Achabhaich and Clachanach respectively. Just north of the cathedral were Camerons and also MacInneses. One of them, Janet, was known as Seonaid nan Tolls because she opened and shut the gate between that area and Clachanach. Whether it had actually operated as a toll-gate at some earlier time is not known.

In the West End the pattern was less settled in succeeding years, as people left and others changed holdings. But along the Sligineach shore we know that there were Lamonts, Macleans, Camerons, Mac-Donalds and MacInneses while on the crofts across the centre were several other MacDonald and MacInnes families. Cùlbhuirg lay within the East End, as the boundary takes a diagonal line following the Glen towards the Machair, and five or six families appear to have been tenants there under the new system. It is not certain where their houses stood as the stones have long since been reused in later buildings, but they were probably grouped together and the arable land divided up among them. It is here that the name MacCormick first appears. Dugald MacCormick came in from the Ross of Mull as tenant and ground officer for the estate when the crofting system began. The making of the crofts led to the custom of identifying someone by adding the name of their holding after their own Christian or full name, for example 'Duncan Achabhaich' or 'Hector Maclean Sligineach'. This was to remain common practice until well into the twentieth century.

Colin Campbell is said to have been given a lot in Cùlbhuirg on his return from serving in the Peninsular Wars. And his wife's father, John Cameron, was a man of some consequence. Cameron's people were from Morvern but many of that clan were on the move in the years after the 1745 campaign, and five families ended up in the Scoor area – four staying in the Ross of Mull and one going to Iona. John was drover to the Duke of Argyll and in the pre-crofting village had the most substantial house, where any officials sent by the Duke would stay. It was called Taigh Bàn na Faiche, the white house of the plain, and stood on the brae near to the nunnery. In the 1980s, descendants Calum Cameron and John Campbell could still tell stories of John Cameron's droving adventures, evading robbers and venturing over the border to Carlisle to get a better price for his cattle, thus earning his nickname Iain Ruadh Sasunnach (red John the Englishman). When in expansive and fanciful mood, another distant relative, Neillie Betsy, had Iain Ruadh going as far as Smithfield!

John Cameron's son Colin will have been allocated a holding in the West End under the new system. He also had the right to cultivate some rigs on Druim Dhùghaill, high moorland in the common pasture area to the south. His grandson Donald could still point them out to his son, Calum, more than a hundred years later. Reasonable though the croft land was in extent and quality, it had to meet the needs of a swiftly growing population who in turn supported the infirm and land-less among them. It was very probably in the early decades of the nineteenth century that all corners capable of producing a crop or a few potatoes were pressed into service.

A school had been established on Iona in 1774 by the Scottish Society for the Propagation of Christian Knowledge and from this period onward schoolmasters feature strongly in the documentary record, as prominent members of the community. Until the island had a resident minister, after the Telford parish church was built in 1828 under the parliamentary scheme to increase the number of churches in the Highlands, the schoolmaster undertook the duties of catechist, Sabbath school teacher and leader of prayer meetings.

He was also one of the few inhabitants who could speak English and so regularly acted as guide to the visitors who flocked to Iona in increasing numbers from the end of the eighteenth century. One who comes vividly to life in several of their journals is 'Ailean Sgoilear', Alan Maclean. Small of stature and round of face, a bonnet of beaver-fur on his head, he led his audience energetically around the ruins and kept a wary eye out for souvenir hunters. For some years he slept with a stone lion from Abbot MacKinnon's tomb under his bed, having appre-hended the would-be thief at the shore.

These guides were imbued with whatever store of tradition was alive on the island at the time but, as they were also literate, the information they conveyed to visitors will have been influenced by written sources which themselves were a mixture of fact, myth and impression. A James Bailey noted in 1787 that the teacher had received from an earlier visitor a copy of an Irish *Life of Columba* – possibly the vernacu-lar adaptation of Adomnán's – written in the twelfth century, and so 'his narrations were not exclusively limited to oral information'. The Norwegian scholar P. A. Munch was in Iona in 1849 and later wrote: 'It cannot be denied that travel accounts, antiquarian writings and so on studied by schoolmasters and *cicerones* have done much damage by mixing the old legends with all sorts of later conjectures and spurious things …'.

The first book to deal with Iona alone, as opposed to the islands in general or St Columba, was *An Historical Account of Iona* by Lachlan Maclean which came out in 1833 and ran to several editions. Alan Maclean had a copy tucked under his arm when Robert Carruthers landed to view the sights in 1835. This book is a prime example of solid documentation, for example extracts from rentals, combined with 'spurious things' such as a description of druidical worship. It also, significantly for the many hundreds it must have influenced, reprinted Dean Monro's suggestion that forty-eight Scottish kings were buried on Iona. So fact and fable continued to weave their many layers around the Sacred Isle.

In 1798 the Revd John Smith from Campbeltown, a well-known clergyman, wrote a book about St Columba or 'Colum Cille the Apostle of the Highlands'. In it he quoted the saying that begins 'In Iona of my heart' and praised the Dukes of Argyll for beginning to fulfil the prophecy that one day 'Iona shall be as it was' by enclosing the grounds with a wall.

Antiquarian interest from the outside did continue to prompt attention from the landowner to the ruins in his care. The Iona Club was founded in 1833 by a number of eminent scholars, including W. F. Skene and Donald Gregory, and they did some excavation work in St Oran's Chapel, bringing to light several grave-slabs hitherto undiscovered. Regrettably, their publishing programme, intended to substitute 'an authentic history' of the Highlands for the 'fables and errors that have so long prevailed', ran to only one volume and after Gregory's premature death in 1836 the Club petered out. Pressure from the Society of Antiquaries in the mid-1850s led to some preservation work and tidying up. It was at this stage that some of the best examples of the carved tombstones were gathered together into two rows and enclosed by iron railings. Major consolidation of both the cathedral and the nunnery ruins was undertaken over several years from 1874 under the direction of architect R. Rowand Anderson.

Local lore, laced with superstition, still attached itself strongly to the religious sites. The granite trough marked with a cross, where pilgrims washed their feet before entering the cathedral, was also known to the natives as the cradle of the wind. By blowing upon the water, a wind could be brought up from any desired direction. Angus Lamont claimed to have seen An Leac Dhubh, the black stone on which solemn oaths were sworn, at the entrance to the cloisters. He described it as about 4 feet high with an effigy of a human figure on the front and so it may have been a grave-slab, endowed with particular reverence. A 'native maniac' was said to have broken it up about 1800 although whether he did so consciously to counter its mythical powers, or because he was himself subject to them, is hard to tell.

A well near to St Mary's Chapel east of the cathedral was thought to have healing properties and a drink from Tobar a' Cheathain was often requested by old people on their deathbed. Holy wells were common in the Highlands and another well-reported Iona custom, the turning of the Clachan Brath or judgement stones, also had parallels elsewhere. Dr Joseph Anderson described these stones to the Society of Antiquaries in 1898, along with accounts of places in Ireland, Islay and Kilberry where he knew of similar small stones, laid on a larger one and turned round to invoke a curse or revenge or healing.

There were many more examples. William Maxwell's book *Iona and the Ionians*, published in 1857, was scathing about such 'absurd and superstitious customs', nurtured during long winter nights spent 'spinning a yarn', and he attributed them to lack of education and to isolation from those parts of the country 'more civilised and enlightened'. What the people thought of him is not recorded. Not for the first nor for the last time was intense interest in the island matched by a similarly high degree of misunderstanding about the culture and way of life of the islanders.

7

Turning-Points

The 1840s brought two crises to the island, neither of them exclusive to Iona but each with its own local impact. The first, following the Disruption within the Church of Scotland in 1843, was the formation of a Free Church congregation led by the incumbent minister Donald McVean. Throughout much of the Highlands the new denomination won mass support among the small tenantry but in Iona nearly half the population remained loyal to the Established Church where a new minister, Alexander MacGregor, was appointed within months.

The rift undoubtedly led to strain between and even within families, a difficulty probably heightened by the fact that Mr McVean was already a prominent and respected personality within the community. A learned man of wide interests, he was a fervent evangelical in the pulpit and a dispenser of practical advice on the ground – on subjects ranging from gardening to education and medical care. Among the antiquarians and theologians he entertained at the manse was the American minister James Richmond, who was happy to record that in September 1849 he saw the roof go on 'the neat little church' at Port nam Mairtear. This ended six years when Mr McVean had had to preach from a wooden 'sentry box' shelter in the open air.

Mr McVean commanded a degree of moral authority also. Richmond noted that he had discouraged 'some barbarous customs' such as excessive intake of alcohol at funerals. Indeed, the local innkeeper had been persuaded to cease the sale of whisky altogether. And both denominations shared strict observance of the Sabbath. An anecdote recounted to the author by Calum Cameron brought this home graphically. It must have happened in the late 1860s when the sappers were on the island, surveying for the first Ordnance Survey map: 'My father was a young boy at the time and he got a seagull from them. They caught a seagull and gave it to him but one Sunday he didn't have any food for it, so he slipped down to the rocks to get limpets. And the Free Church elders saw him and reported him to his grandfather – I don't think he ever forgot it!'

Dissension in the spiritual life of the island, however, was soon over-taken by an economic and social disaster that spared no one. Blight struck the potato crop with crippling severity, its spores borne indis-criminately on the damp air, leaving behind them blackened fields and a rotten stench. The year 1846 came to be remembered as 'a'bhliadhna a dh'fhalbh am buntàta' – the year the potato went away.

On 25 December, not in any case a day of special celebration in the Highlands at that time, Mr MacGregor wrote from the Established Church manse on Iona that 'the poor here are in a state of great desti-tution … prospects in regard to the spring and summer are dark and dismal'. In fact, there followed a decade of acute hardship in much of the Hebrides and western mainland, and the financial collapse which subsequently threatened many estates precipitated a wave of clearance and emigration.

In common with many other areas, Iona's population had spiralled rapidly upwards in the early decades of the nineteenth century. It reached probably its highest figure of 521 in 1835. The island's good land notwithstanding, these were a lot of mouths to feed. Meanwhile, previously reliable sources of additional income – seasonal migration, kelping – were contracting, crop failures in the late 1830s had already put a strain on local resources and there was too much dependence on the potato. Government food relief eased the immediate impact of the famine, and public works – such as drainage or building roads and a jetty – generated a little cash for which meal could be purchased. Assistance with fares, from the estate or from the Highland and Island Emigration Society, persuaded many to emigrate to North America, Australia or New Zealand.

John Campbell from Islay came on stage at this crucial period, as the Duke's factor – 'Am Factor Mòr' – for the Ross of Mull, Iona and Tiree. 'Bha e trom oirnn dar a bha e san t-saoghal agus tha e trom oirnn an diugh' said the men carrying his coffin twenty-five years later: 'He was heavy on us when he was in this world and he is heavy on us today.' At his door, certainly, was laid blame for the hefty rent rise of 50 per cent which the Iona crofters had to meet in 1847 while they were still struggling with the effects of the potato failure. Their extreme difficulty in doing so led ultimately to the evidence they were to present, through their spokesman Malcolm Ferguson, to the Napier Commission of 1883. Iona was one of only six crofting areas examined by the commissioners where high rent, rather than access to land, was at the heart of the people's grievances. Tensions between tenantry and estate did not finally subside until the Crofters Act of 1886 brought security of tenure and the opportunity to win a reduction in rents.

Behind Clachanach croft, the mossy surface of the Lochan Mòr – which served as a mill pond for the monks – is etched today with deep straight lines, the drainage ditches which John MacArthur dug during the potato famine years. He left another legacy of that time when, on a June day in 1847, he was at Port Rònain to see ninety-eight people leave Iona for a new life overseas. Ever since, his descendants have passed on that very precise, very stark statistic. Today it would mean that almost the entire population was to gather on the jetty, with a trunk or a few boxes of belongings. A century and a half ago it represented about one-fifth of the inhabitants but was none the less traumatic for that. It was the biggest single exodus within memory, possibly the only one of such a size that the close-knit community had ever experienced.

There had already been a trickle outwards over many years and the names of a few who left, usually of their own volition, have come down in a variety of ways. 'Chaidh air thuras na chèutabh do Iamaica air aineol – he has gone joyfully on a voyage, on a vessel to Jamaica' is a line from a poem by Angus Lamont, probably composed in the early years of the nineteenth century, lamenting the departure for the West Indies of a friend called Neil Morison. The nickname Niall a' Rudha, Neil of the point, recalls a MacFarlane who had a small house on the shoreline below Clachanach and was one of the first to emigrate to Canada. Calum Cameron knew that a number of his own relatives later stayed with these MacFarlanes when they went out to begin a new life.

Calum was also aware that his own father, Donald, had fully expected to go too towards the end of the nineteenth century and had sent his trunk on ahead. But for some reason he never received definite word and the unclaimed trunk was eventually sent back across the Atlantic. It sat in the barn at Traighmòr for years, apparently, a reminder of a journey that never was. Had Donald gone he would doubtless have taken part in the impressive family gathering of sixty adults and twenty-eight children which took place at Thistleton, Ontario in 1930, all descendants of two half-brothers from Iona, John Black and Colin Cameron.

At Clachanach too, fate played its part. Family letters have shown that a Neil MacArthur went from there to Australia, probably in the 1830s, but he lost touch early on. Thirty years later a new settler from Mull, a brother-in-law of Mr McVean, met up with him and sent his address back to Iona. Neil's nephew Dugald wrote with the news from home and, although he had heard Australia was 'a wild and ungodly place', revealed that he had considered going there himself. But the brothers of his generation at Clachanach had died young and so there was no one else to keep up the croft.

Over the two middle decades of the century, Iona's population dropped by nearly half. Three farms were created by amalgamating vacated crofts and some previously congested holdings had thinned out. At Achabhaich, for example, there were three families at the census of 1841 but by 1861 there was only one, the tenant Duncan MacArthur. His sister Catherine and husband Alexander MacDonald had accepted two pounds of estate assistance for themselves and their seven children, to board the *Barlow* bound for Canada in 1849. Duncan's brother James had operated as general merchant for a few years at Achabhaich but took the chance of his own croft at Sligineach in 1859, after Alexander Black left there for New Zealand.

Despite the dislocation – and the very real suffering – of the potato famine years, the crofting community created by the fifth Duke of Argyll kept its foothold on the island. Had he not made the reforms he did, and had Iona still been under the runrig system yielding inadequate returns during this period of crisis, then its subsequent story

might well have been different. It is not improbable that the eighth
Duke and his Factor Mòr might have been tempted to take the opportunity to sweep away the clustered village by the ruins and allocate all
of Iona's green acres, to one or two farmers.

Combing the beach for anything that might be of use is an age-old
occupation of coastal and island dwellers. As in the day of the monks,
the sea continued to bring both risk and opportunity. There were
at least four shipwrecks close to Iona over the winter of 1848–9, at
the height of the potato famine, when anything remotely edible
that floated ashore – in one lucky case a cask of pork – was swiftly
appropriated.

Over the years the names of many vessels were to enter island lore.
There was the *Graf von Sklifen* at Sandeels Bay and the *St Peter*, somewhere on the south coast, whose crew scrambled ashore and met Flora
Cameron milking cattle in the hills. In 1881 a visitor, John Stewart,
took a trip round the island in John MacDonald's boat, during which
they salvaged planks from the recently wrecked *Minnie Knapp*. She
was scuttled, they say, after hitting a rock off Canna, limping towards
Iona and then dumping her cargo of limestone in Sloc Strath Mugain,
the same gully where the *Troubador* of Belfast had come to grief the
winter before.

John MacDonald was then the official guide and recounted to
Stewart the fate of the American schooner *Guy Mannering* on the last
day of 1865, probably the most poignant tragedy of all. Dugald
MacArthur was stranded at Fionnphort by the same fierce gale that
swept the stricken ship on to the Machair shore. He saw her three
masts on the skyline and could only imagine the frantic rescue efforts
in which he was unable to help. The islanders formed a human chain,
as far as they dared into the lashing waves, and brought nineteen
passengers and crew to safety. Their bravery was later rewarded by
medals and testimonials from the Royal Humane Society. The survivors were cared for in local homes and the fifteen who drowned were
given a dignified burial in the Reilig Odhráin.

The drama lived long in local tradition. There was the story of
the rescuers pulling out of the water one limp form who spluttered
a few words of relief. 'Tha Gàidhlig aig an fhear seo!' they said in

astonishment, 'This one speaks Gaelic!' and then they recognised John
Campbell, the West End shepherd. There was small Mary Ann
MacCormick from the village running out of a neighbour's house,
startled by the unexpected sight of a black sailor sitting up in bed. And
that particularly stormy winter brought much public pressure for a
lighthouse, not least from Neil MacKay, the Iona correspondent for
the *North British Daily Mail*. In 1867, work finally began on Dhu
Heartach, to provide a beacon on the treacherous Torran Rocks south-
east of Iona. Many links were to be forged between the island and the
new community of lighthouse builders, and then keepers, which was
set up on Erraid off the tip of the Ross of Mull.

The population remained stable for the remainder of the nineteenth
century and in 1891 stood at 247, about three-quarters of them living
on the farms and crofts. The schoolroom was bursting at the seams
with over eighty pupils, about 40 per cent of whom were boarded-out
children from Glasgow. The practice whereby city parochial boards
placed orphans or abandoned children with guardians in rural areas
had worked well in Iona, first for a spell in the 1860s and then again
from the early 1880s.

An influx of day visitors from yachts or steamships was already
another familiar sight each summer, now regularly augmented by
those who chose to stay for longer, in the two hotels or in houses let
by the islanders. Guidebooks proliferated, shells and 'lucky' green
pebbles were preferred enthusiastically by local youngsters at make-
shift stalls and the Iona Press set up shop in a bothy opposite the St
Columba Hotel. This was the brainchild of John MacCormick from
Tormore in the Ross of Mull and William Muir, former manager of
the granite quarry there who had already founded a private press in
Edmonton, north London, making fine facsimiles of the poetic works
of William Blake. The booklets they produced on Iona over their few
years of operation were mostly illustrated versions of Gaelic poems and
folklore. These had the conscious aim of recalling 'the island's ancient
glory' as a seat of great scholarship, where monks and craftsmen had
once laboured to leave for posterity manuscripts and crosses of
enduring beauty.

Round the fireside, however, it seemed that tales of monks and saints had now been put aside. 'Cha robh mòran iomraidh air Calum Cille aig cèilidh' wrote the Revd Coll A. MacDonald, born in 1873 on a croft at Machair: 'There was not much talk of Columba in the ceilidh house.' His memories, rather, were full of boyhood hours spent listening to sparky debates over crofting rights in the smiddy, of stories in the weaver's house about how Dr Johnson soaked himself jumping impatiently ashore at Port Rònain and of the exploits of Dòmhnull Dròbhair, a famous Mull cattle drover, on the road to Falkirk. He called these gatherings 'sgoil-oidhche ar n-athraichean', our fore-fathers' night-school, where there was everything from music to mirth, from riddles to ancient history.

Sitting at the feet of the old folk certainly honed his own ability to retell the traditions and recapture the experiences of his youth. In a letter to a son by then in America, Coll eloquently recreated the atmosphere of a January day in 1881 when, for the last time as it turned out, crowds gathered for the New Year shinty match on a flat stretch of Machair just above where the Atlantic breakers swish rhythmically on to the gravel of Ceann na Creige. The event had been eagerly anticipated – 'For weeks the youth played shinty, talked shinty, dreamed shinty' as they made their camans from the hazel woods of the Ross of Mull. Captains were Donald MacDonald, Coll's father and 'massive as a Viking', pitted against the small, swift and wiry Richard Sinclair of Maol farm. A shinty was tossed in the air to the shout of 'cas no bas' – 'head or handle' – to decide the direction of play and the chosen teams streamed out.

'I can still see two bearded warriors on the sea side of the plain' wrote Coll, 'whose speed filled my boyish eyes with wonder. They were Calum Cameron and his cousin John Campbell … in their stocking soles their fast runs made a magnificent spectacle … like Achilles and Hector on the plains of Troy, first the one and then the other prevailed.' Eventually, as the light waned and shinty sticks were smashed into splinters, the great game finished in a draw. Coll's recollections included the night of celebrations, as the bottle went up and down the table followed by tales of bygone matches and heroes, and 'song and story chased each other to the end of a perfect day'.

Life was by no means constant recreation and conviviality. But these occasions were important and the ties of custom and kinship which underpinned them were strong factors binding a society of this kind together. That many who emerged from such a community were also articulate, well informed and outward-looking would no doubt have come as a surprise to the William Maxwells who judged their culture 'primitive' and of limited scope. This book's companion volume mentions a number of locals who excelled in various ways, including Donald A. MacDonald who guided George Washington Wilson around the Iona ruins, Neil MacKay tailor, newspaper correspondent and razor-sharp wit, and Malcolm Ferguson who read through every volume in the encyclopaedia donated to the island's library.

Another who was well read on events of the day, and knowledgeable too about old ways and beliefs, was Alexander MacInnes, or Alastair Ruanaich to follow the local habit of naming people after their croft. Through him has come down a curious incident, touching perhaps on something very old. It happened about the 1880s at Cùldamph one February night when Kate Campbell felt unwell. She drank the water her husband had gone to fetch from the well and asked him: 'Where did you get the wine? try it, it tastes like wine.' According to her grandson John Campbell, from whom the author recorded this story in 1992, the mystery was not solved until Alastair Ruanaich came in the next morning to ask how she was and found her much improved. 'O, thuirt esan, b'e sin Oidhche Fheill Finnein, a chaidh an t-uisge a thionndaidh na fhìon agus thachair gun do bhuail sibh air a' bhlasad an uair sin' – 'Oh, he said, that was St Finnan's eve, when the water turned to wine and you happened to catch a taste of it.'

There are clear biblical connotations here, in the miracle at the wedding in Cana, and Colum Cille too is credited with drawing water from a well that then turned into wine for the Eucharist. This is said to have happened while he was with Bishop Findbarr in Ireland. And there may be a link with Oidhch' Inid, the night of Shrove Tuesday, which has been found to transmute into Oidhch' Fhinnein – Finnan's night – in some traditions.

The local ministers might well have looked upon such throw-backs to ancient beliefs with some disfavour. The veneration of saints was firmly renounced by the Presbyterian faith, even on Colum Cille's own island. The people may have had a keen interest in him and his monastery as subjects of historical interest, as also did ministers such as Donald McVean and Archibald MacMillan who came to the Established Church charge in 1890. But it is highly unlikely that the saint retained any spiritual significance for the people in the way that had perhaps still been evident a century before when Dr Walker made his remarks.

Alongside this ran a deep suspicion of other denominations, particularly of the Roman Catholics and the Episcopalians. There was quite a stir in 1848, according to eyewitness Henry Graham, when Alexander Ewing, Episcopal Bishop of Argyll and the Isles, preached amid the cathedral ruins. For the Bishop it was deeply moving to be where 'for so long a time and from so remote a period the gospel sounded forth' and to hear nothing there now but the wild bird's cry. He ended with the prophecy attributed to the saint, 'An I mo chridhe, an I mo ghràidh … In Iona of my heart, Iona of my love …'. Graham's wry observation was that this was given in the original Gaelic 'for the benefit of the wretched cast-away Presbyterians' forming the outer circle. Mr McVean was reportedly furious.

In 1892, Mr MacMillan worked up a righteous rage, and a petition, when a successor of Ewing, Bishop Alexander Chinnery-Haldane, applied to the Duke of Argyll for permission to erect a retreat house and chapel on Iona. It was built in the end, in 1894, and is the only spot on the island with a statue of St Columba, set on its eastern wall gazing out across the Sound.

In June 1897, the *Oban Times* editorial, under the heading 'A flash of concord at Iona' praised the courtesy and good feeling which had characterised the recent celebrations of the 1300th anniversary of Columba's death. But 'a chance for the Millenium was missed' through the insistence by Presbyterian, Episcopalian and Catholic churchmen that they hold three separate events. There ought, the paper felt, to be one combined service on such occasions: 'All may therefore commemorate him but none may claim him as their own. The most that can be said is that he was of the church of his time and we are safe in honouring him for what he did as a pioneer of religion and education.' The Duke of Argyll was not deaf to mild rebukes of this kind, as events were to show within a couple of years.

Across the water in Ireland, too, the anniversary was marked by widespread demonstrations of devotion, at the saint's birthplace in

Gartan, at Durrow and at Derry, where 'extraordinary religious feeling' was reported in the city. Mass was said at the Long Tower, the spot where the Doire Chaluim Cille, Colum Cille's oak grove, was said to stand. And crowds flocked to take away bottles of water from his well, closed off for some years and reopened for the occasion.

Events great and small, national and local, made their mark on island life in the closing years of the century, as a flick through the pages of the *Oban Times* reveals. Three puffers discharged their cargo of coal at Port nam Mairtear in the same week in 1898, 'an unprecedented thing', but there was concern at the poor state of the Port Rònain slipway, vital for the landing of all other goods. Lobster fishing was flourishing but crops suffered due to gales and heavy rain during September 1899. A regatta, the first for fifteen years, was revived in 1897 and a committee was set up to manage the Machair golf course, increasingly popular with visitors and locals.

Celebrations for the Diamond Jubilee of Queen Victoria that same year followed a month after those for the Columban anniversary. The children headed for a day of games on the Machair, led by piper Duncan MacDonald Ardionra who, although only 13, was already a talented player and had been given a set of pipes by Lord Archibald Campbell. At night a bonfire was made on Dùn I and lit by John Black, the oldest man present, and a Jubilee Cairn was planned for the summit of this the island's highest hill.

A message was sent to the Queen, and a reply received from her private secretary, courtesy of the telegraph service installed in the spring of 1897 in the new Post Office, built on the village brae by Angus MacPhail. On the day the service opened, sixty-six telegrams were sent – one of the first, in Gaelic, from Mr Dewar the Free Church minister to Mr Munro, ironmonger in Oban. With admirable business acumen, Angus nailed a notice outside for the summer season: 'Wire your friends from the Holy Isle'. Delivering a telegram in return for a few pence soon became a common job for local youngsters.

The MacPhail family had come from Torosay in Mull in 1848, to the new farm holdings of Cùlbhuirg and then Maol. Angus went to sea but returned home in 1896 to take over the Post Office from the MacDonald family two generations of whom had run it since the service began in 1851. And in December 1897 the new postmaster married Marion MacArthur from Clachanach. Weddings were the occasions, above all, when the community came together in celebration. Someone, very possibly Angus's great friend Alexander Ritchie whose family had come to the Columba Hotel and farm in 1868, sent a lively account of the festivities to the newspaper:

> We had a genuine Highland marriage ... To the strains of several pipers the company marched from the abodes of the bride and groom to the prettily lit-up church, the entrance to which – out of compliment to the groom's hitherto maritime connection – was clearly shown by a port and starboard light. The ringing of bells, the firing of guns and rockets burst on the ears of the party as they filed out of the church on their way to the schoolhouse where to the inspiring strains of the pipes and fiddle the light fantastic toe was tripped for several hours. After the dance the party marched to the house of the bride where, after a sumptuous supper, song and story and hearty good wishes for the young couple ended a day which will be long remembered in Iona.

Figure 3 Angus and Marion MacPhail, a few years after their wedding in 1897, at the back of Block House – the cottage Angus built up to two storeys, and named while the Boer War was still underway. Photograph courtesy of Antonia Maclean; taken by her mother Elsie M. Ogilvie, a regular visitor to Iona.

Part Three

*Ach mun tig an saoghal
gu crìch
But ere the world shall
come to an end*

8

A Cathedral Restored

On 22 September 1899 a group of the country's most distinguished academics and churchmen gathered in the Church of Scotland's offices at 123 George Street in Edinburgh. The moderator, the Right Revd John Pagan, opened the proceedings with prayer. Around the table were Sir John Cheyne (Church of Scotland Procurator), the Very Revd R. H. Story (principal of Glasgow University), Sir William Muir (principal of Edinburgh University), Sir William Geddes (principal of Aberdeen University), the Very Revd J. Cameron Lees of St Giles Cathedral and the Revd Pearson McAdam Muir of St Mungoes Cathedral. Also invited, but unable to be present, was principal Alexander Stewart of St Mary's College, St Andrews University.

This was the first meeting of the Iona Cathedral Trustees. The Duke of Argyll had decided to relinquish ownership of the cathedral and nunnery ruins and the Reilig Odhráin and transfer them into the care of a public trust linked to the Church of Scotland. The trustees were appointed, not in a personal capacity but by virtue of the offices they held – in Scotland's four ancient universities, in the cathedrals of Edinburgh and Glasgow and in the Established Church itself. Clearly it was designed to be a national body of some permanent standing.

The Duke's official reasoning was that Iona's historic sites were of interest to the whole nation, indeed to the Christian community everywhere, and that their future would be better secured in public hands rather than subject to the whims of fortune of a single family. The news was only made public when several newspapers carried the full text of the Deed of Trust on 30 September 1899, but it is clear from family memoirs that the idea had been gestating for some time. The Revd Dr James MacGregor of St Cuthbert's in Edinburgh wrote enthusiastically to Lady Victoria Campbell about 'this great and splendid gift to the Church', recalling that he had put such a suggestion to her father as long as twenty-two years before, after a discussion which had also included Dr Story. This must have been soon after the Duke was first inspired by Dr MacGregor's preaching, marking the start of a long and close personal friendship between them.

The new trustees wrote to the Duke to express their deep sense of honour at the responsibility vested in them and their view that 'all patriotic Scotsmen and Presbyterians' would support his wish that the cathedral be restored for public worship. This declared aim was central to the Deed of Trust. Many of those present at the 1897 services of celebration under the temporary roof had already made appeals that a permanent rebuilding be considered. And there was an important extra clause, specifying that not only Scots and Presbyterians be allowed to hold services there, but members of all other Christian churches too. Perhaps the Duke wished to bring to an end the murmerings of discontent from the Protestant community on previous occasions when Roman Catholic pilgrimages to Iona had requested a place to worship. Moreover, there had been clear hints in Irish Catholic journals of the time that the Catholic Church wished to secure the island for themselves, a step which might have considerably fuelled such discontent. And doubtless he wished to pre-empt any echoes of the recent controversy with the Episcopal Church over the erection of its retreat house and chapel. Not that he regarded other denominations with any special warmth, and in a letter to Lady Victoria he freely admitted that neither the Roman Catholic nor Anglican Churches would like his decision.

The decision, however, was now made and the task of restoration had to begin. But no endowment had come with the gift. The trustees were going to have to raise every penny from scratch. William J. Menzies, the Edinburgh lawyer appointed to act as agent for the Trust, visited the island in 1900 and recommended some initial minor work, such as setting a concrete platform under the ridges of the chiefs and kings – which had become uneven – and railing off grave-slabs in the nunnery. An appeal for money did not get off the ground until 1901, as it was felt there were already enough demands for public subscriptions while the Boer War continued. A little cash was raised directly from visitors by putting up a collection box, which brought in an average of about £60 for the first few seasons. Mr Menzies agreed to continue the engagement of Alex Ritchie as guide and custodian and his annual fee of £25 was more than covered by the £50 contribution made by David MacBrayne, in return for the free access of his passengers to the ruins. MacBrayne also permitted the display of a notice and box on the steamer, inviting support for the restoration project.

Finally, early in 1902, plans were submitted by architects MacGibbon and Ross of Edinburgh for the roofing of the choir, the tower, the south aisle and transept and the glazing of the windows. This was all carried out that summer at a cost of £2,750. Regrettably, the eighth Duke did not live to see this first stage in the fulfilment of his wishes. Before his death in 1900 he had placed on record his own hope that the rebuilding would conform as closely as possible to the original, even including replacement of the cap-shaped structure on top of the tower, 'as it was peculiar'.

He was also, however, spared involvement in the ensuing controversy over what was or was not authentic, to which any restoration work is inevitably vulnerable. His own daughter, Lady Frances Balfour, was critical of the interior oak roof and of the general standard of the masonry work. Others found the replacement window in the south aisle out of harmony, a view shared by Dr Story on a visit in 1904. The original stone tracery was considered too eroded to be capable of restoration, although it was removed to St Conan's Church on Loch Awe where it may still be seen.

Otherwise, Dr Story remained a staunch proponent of the trustees' task and in an article in *Scottish Arts and Letters* of 1903 he chided as selfish those who resisted change of any kind. A typical reaction in this vein had come almost as soon as the Trust was formed, in a letter dated October 1899 from archaeologist J. Romilly Allan to G. Baldwin Brown, professor of Fine Arts at Edinburgh University. Allan hoped there would be no 'tinkering' with Iona Cathedral as its chief attraction for artists lay in 'its ruinous and desolate appearance'. Nor was Baldwin Brown reticent about expressing grave reservations over the restoration, as newspaper correspondence of the time showed. The questions were aired as far afield as the *London Chronicle*, where an anonymous piece – perhaps penned by one of these gentlemen – ended up with the blunt assertion that 'anything done to these ruins beyond what may be necessary to preserve them from falling to pieces would be a grievous blunder'.

Nevertheless, the trustees held to their task. By 1903 Glasgow architect John Honeyman had been engaged to work along with MacGibbon and Ross and it was he who supervised the completion of the north transept and sacristy and various further repairs to masonry and windows up to the end of the next year. A new wall was built around the Reilig Odhráin, contracted locally to Coll MacDonald and John MacCallum. A number of skilled tradesmen from Mull were employed during the restoration, including the MacCallums, a well-known stonemason family from Kentra, and the Grahams, joiners from Bunessan.

The trustees' report to the General Assembly in 1904 noted that fund-raising had been disappointingly slow, despite the best efforts of the committee led by the Revd Donald MacLeod, formerly of St Columba's Church in London. They had perhaps been hampered by the initial burst of adverse criticism. It was acknowledged, too, that the public might be unclear about the eventual aim of the restoration but expressed the hope that 'in time the Cathedral may become the regular place of worship for the people of Iona'.

This was a significant and tactful statement. Local reaction to the setting up of the Trust, and to its plan of work, is not recorded but the islanders had a long-standing link with the buildings since the times they gathered within the ruined walls for Sunday prayers, before the present parish church was erected. From among their ranks were drawn guides who knew the history of the historic sites and who had kept alive many of the stories associated with them.

Yet in his Deed of Trust the Duke had expressly excluded the parish minister and Kirk Session of Iona from involvement in management of the sites or worship in the cathedral. Embedded in the clause was the phrase 'for the time being', lending weight to the theory that it was prompted by irritation with the then minister, Archibald MacMillan, over recent controversies such as that over the Episcopal retreat. One sharp-eyed writer to *The Scotsman* in October 1899 pointed out the ambivalence of this, since a minister could legally prevent the intrusion of another into his parish. Unwittingly, he was anticipating a future, keenly felt dispute.

On 14 July 1905, however, Mr MacMillan led his parishioners, and a congregation swelled to 300 by visitors and guests, in the singing of the 100th psalm to open the first service in the restored cathedral church. Also present was the Dowager Duchess of Argyll, who had earlier donated funds to cover the cost of decorating the south transept. It was undoubtedly a great occasion for the island and, with the loan of chairs and a pulpit from the Highland and Home Mission Committee, the parish services were continued in the cathedral throughout that summer.

The trustees pressed on with their public appeal but further work had to be put on hold until this bore fruit. The minutes record one or two setbacks in 1907, first of all through the deaths of Sir John Cheyne and Dr Story, both venerated churchmen and both strongly committed to the Iona Cathedral Trust. John Honeyman resigned as architect, owing to advancing years, but there was brighter news from Miss Helen Campbell of Blythswood. She and her brother Walter had already made a generous loan to the Trust at the start of the appeal. Now, through contacts with the Church of Scotland Woman's Guilds, she had organised a committee of ladies to raise funds, at home and abroad, for completion of the cathedral nave. Within two years this single-minded effort brought a handsome reward of £1,500 into the Trust's coffers and the newly appointed architect P. MacGregor Chalmers was able to begin work in 1909. The first service in the fully restored cathedral church was on 26 June 1910, led by two of the trustees, Dr McAdam Muir of Glasgow Cathedral and Sir Donald MacAlister, principal of Glasgow University.

The generosity of donors was marked in a variety of ways. The east window of the aisle had been paid for by and was dedicated to Miss Campbell, while in the nave the west window became a memorial to the Revd Dr Robert Blair, who had for many years been responsible for the Highland Mission within the Church of Scotland. The large south window had been funded by the Highlanders of Nova Scotia and a teak board, carved and painted in Celtic lettering by Alex Ritchie,

was placed beneath it as a gesture of gratitude. A service of dedication
for gifts to the cathedral, in July 1913, served as another reminder of
the wide circle of supporters that the restoration work had eventually
attracted. These included Professor R. A. S. McAlister of Cambridge
who gave one oak door, for the vestry, and the Grant family from
Canada who gave another; Messrs Bell from Dundee who gave the
pulpit, and the widow and daughter of the late moderator Dr Theodore
Marshall, who gave the font. The daughters of the late Dr Story
presented the pulpit Bible in memory of their father.

In 1912 a white marble effigy of the eighth Duke of Argyll, designed
by Sir George Frampton, was unveiled in the south transept. This
was at the request of Ina, the Dowager Duchess and her own statue
was placed alongside a few years later. And on a wild day at the very
close of 1925 she was brought on her last journey to Iona. Archibald
MacArthur needed eight men on the oars of his big skiff to bring the
funeral party ashore from the steamer *Princess Louise*, on charter from

Figure 4   Funeral party of Ina Duchess of Argyll approaching the Cathedral
door, with local men carrying the coffin, December 1925.

Oban. Tenants loaded the wreaths into a cart and carried the coffin to the cathedral where Duchess Ina was buried beneath her own effigy. The south transept remains a memorial to the last of the Argyll family to own the historic building.

The Established Church congregation on Iona adopted the new place of worship with enthusiasm. With the consent of the trustees, the summer services begun in 1905 were continued and, from about 1913, were held there during the winter also. The large numbers of visitors attending in summer certainly justified the move to the larger space. A clear childhood memory of these Sundays for Mary MacArthur was being shepherded with other children on to the chilly stone steps below the altar as the pews filled up to capacity.

Special celebrations, too, cemented the islanders' renewed relationship with the cathedral. On 11 March 1909 Janet MacNiven Maol married Archibald MacArthur Clachanach. The wedding, conducted entirely in Gaelic, was hailed by the *Oban Times* as the first in the ancient cathedral for 300 years. (It may well have been the first ever as in pre-Reformation days marriages would have been conducted in the parish church of St Ronan or, possibly, from a house.) In August the same year, a special steamer from Oban brought guests to the wedding in Iona Cathedral of Florence Stanford and the Revd James Cameron, brother of artist D. Y. Cameron.

One discordant note had been struck between the Trust and the islanders, however, almost from the start. It is impossible to know when local burials began in the Reilig Odhráin but by this time the latter had long been the only one among several sites once used. On Mr Menzies' first visit in 1900 he was sensitive to this fact, reporting that burial of their kindred in the graveyard was 'regarded as an immemorial right' by the people and that it would be imprudent to question this. On the other hand, it *was* within the trustees' rights to regulate the use of the ground and he put up a notice stating that all applications to erect tombstones should now be made through the offical custodian, Alex Ritchie. Built into this new rule was the trustees' decision that only horizontal stones be allowed, on the grounds that recumbent slabs were more in keeping with old West Highland tradition. Understandably, perhaps, there was some indignation that the personal choice of a tombstone should be subject to outside authority and the matter rumbled on for a number of years. At a crowded public meeting in 1908 the locals even considered resorting to legal advice after workmen sent by the trustees tried to remove a vertical stone erected to John Campbell Cùldamph. A news item sent to the *Oban Times* by local correspondent Hector Maclean stated that 'a strong feeling has been felt in the island with regard to the actions of the Trustees'. Eventually the stone was replaced, the regulations were drawn up again in Gaelic and English – for circulation to every household – and, with the passage of time, came to be accepted.

Many years later, another decision was to prove unpopular with some, both on and off the island, namely the removal of the carved stones from the familiar 'Ridges' of the kings and chiefs to the cloisters and museum, for their protection from the elements. Air pollution is a relatively modern concern, although a very real one, but the risk of excessive weathering from exposure had already been noted by Mr Menzies on his very first visit in 1900. And his recommendation that sooner or later the stones ought to be placed under cover was echoed by Dr Story four years later.

The trustees did recognise that local involvement in the historic sites was not simply helpful but provided important continuity with past practice. In addition to continuing the employment of Alex Ritchie as custodian, they engaged as caretaker Coll MacDonald whose brother John and father Archibald had acted as guides during the Argyll ownership of the buildings. In turn, Coll was succeeded in the early 1930s by his son Willie and his daughter Annie was appointed as cathedral bell-ringer. The bell was to be tolled at least once each Sunday.

The services of Alex Ritchie, in particular, must have been invaluable because of his knowledge, his easy rapport with visitors and his standing in the community. From 1914 until 1930 he volunteered to go on guiding in an honorary capacity and the trustees reciprocated this generosity by waiving rent on his stall in the nunnery precincts. In 1900 Alex had sought Mr Menzies' permission, which was granted, to continue the craft business which he and his wife had set up, selling their own products along with cheaper trinkets, such as 'Iona marble' souvenirs. These were actually manufactured in Birmingham from Connemara marble, a form of minor hoodwinking designed no doubt to give the customers what they wanted. A few years later, after a brief resurgence of commercial quarrying made suitable quantities of local marble more accessible, the Iona stone was also used. At first glance it is not all that easy to tell the difference.

The Ritchies' work, however, was undeniably authentic and of consistently fine quality. Alex had returned home in the 1890s after a serious leg injury, in a shipwreck in the West Indies, cut short his career with the Merchant Navy. In 1898 he married Euphemia Thomson, who had studied at Glasgow School of Art, and together they developed a keen interest in Celtic design. Alex began by translating this into the wood-carving he had learned at sea and soon extended the skill into raised metalwork in brass, copper and silver. Euphemia specialised in leather and cloth, teaching a number of local women who themselves became adept at making bags, purses and embroidery. In winter the couple regularly attended classes in Glasgow to widen their knowledge of Celtic arts and crafts, studying facsimiles of the *Book of Kells* and the *Book of Lindisfarne* and the complex patterns on the Pictish stones of north-east Scotland.

The range of items in their shop was truly extraordinary: from large mirrors and firescreens through sconces, boxes, trays, plaques and crosses to a huge variety of brooches, buckles, clasps, bracelets, pendants, earrings, paper knives, spoons and trinkets. Some of the silverware was enamelled, in jewel-like colours. Items that proved particularly popular were produced in large numbers while others were unique, perhaps commissioned for a special occasion such as a presentation. The local Boys Club had Ritchie medallions made for their members. As demand increased, production was farmed out to Darby's of Birmingham for the silverwork, and Lawson's of Glasgow for the brass.

The initial and prime inspiration of course was the rich harvest of carved grave-slabs and crosses on Iona, with which Alex Ritchie was thoroughly familiar as custodian and guide. Over the years, in articles and talks, the couple spoke out strongly for far greater recognition of Celtic art in Scottish schools. In the magazine *An Deo-Greine* of 1906 they argued that teaching these ancient forms was an ideal way to instil the first principles of all good design. Moreover, such training might bring out in young people that 'aptitude and instinct for handling tools' inherent in the Celtic race and so provide more of them with an

Figure 5   Alexander and Euphemia Ritchie in the nunnery grounds, 1930s.
Photograph by courtesy of the Russell Trust and St Andrews University
Library.

additional and useful occupation. 'At present, examples of Celtic
design are as foreign to the Highland child as to the Cockney, even in
places where the old monuments can be seen daily', they continued
and, after a plea that these same monuments be adequately protected
for the future, they ended on a note which strikes an uncannily
contemporary chord: 'When it is a question of preserving the art of
other countries, the response is hearty and spontaneous and yet we
view with indifference the decay of our own.'

The erosion of the stones was paralleled, in the Ritchies' minds, by
the potential erosion of a native artistic tradition. Thanks to their
interest and skill, however, this tradition was reinterpreted for a wider
audience and Ritchie pieces remain appreciated and prized to this
day. They form a genuine link back to the craftsmen who flourished on
Iona, and elsewhere in the kingdoms of the Picts and the Scots, more
than a thousand years ago.

9

The New Century

It was not the transfer of the historic ruins alone that seemed to pre-occupy the eighth Duke in his last years. In May 1900, an advertisement in the *Oban Times* indicated that he was prepared to consider applications for feus, long leases or purchases of portions of the island of Iona. Nothing changed hands, however. He may have intended, had he lived, to pursue this course of giving up part of the land, but his son and successor took a much more definite step in 1903 by putting the whole island up for sale. There was one newspaper rumour that 'a gentleman' was interested in purchase and another that French Carthusian monks were behind the negotiations but again nothing came of it. The people of Iona entered a third century as tenants of the House of Argyll.

The Census of 1901 recorded a total of 213 people living in Iona and a decade later the number had moved only a little, up to 222. The pattern on the land was virtually unchanged, too; alongside the three farms, seventeen crofters remained on their holdings.

On the farthest-flung croft, Calva, turf had begun to encroach on the footings of the two houses and stackyard wall, deserted since the MacDonald family emigrated to Canada in 1888. Its good grazing continued to be used, at first by the East End crofters in common and then by the Clachanach MacArthurs, to whom it was assigned in 1904, but it is the only one of the original holdings where any house at all has ceased to be occupied. From these 13 acres on the island's northern rim, the MacDonalds went on to own the 600 acres of Iona Farm at

Fairmount in Manitoba, with six pairs of horses and ninety head
of cattle.

Commenting in 1905, the *Oban Times* added 'This we suppose is
an instance of the many which may be told of the success of the
Highlanders in the far west.' The previous year, the paper had also
recorded the visit back to Iona of Lachlan MacQuarrie, who had emigrated as a boy about 1851 with his father, a shoemaker, and was now
a prosperous farmer in Eldon, Victoria County in Ontario. These were
attractive reports and a trickle of islanders continued to board the
steamers which, with increasing regularity, were sailing west from the
Clyde. In the years up to 1910, Archie and Coll MacCormick and
their sister Flora went out to Manitoba, as did Maggie MacArthur
and her husband, to be joined in Winnipeg a few years later by her
sister Johann. Their brother John also left in 1912, going to Alberta to
continue his career as a banker which he had begun in the Clydesdale
Bank in Tobermory.

The last family to emigrate together were the MacDonalds of Sandbank croft, Sligineach. Sandy had gone out in 1902, trying Saskatche-
wan first and then settling at Basswood in Manitoba from where, over
the next two years, he was able to send home the fare for his widowed
mother Flora and seven brothers and sisters. The eldest daughter, also
Flora, remained in Iona to marry Donald Black of Clachancorrach. It
was a fresh start for the family whom tragedy had struck in 1888 when
John MacDonald was accidentally killed by his own gun. The close-knit
community of emigrants in this part of Manitoba at this time, from
Tiree as well as Iona, will have eased the transition to a new life. Herb
Cooper, born in 1913 to Catherine MacDonald, gives a vivid glimpse
of this in a letter written eighty years later:

> When I was very young I can remember the 'Iona Crowd' –
> clansmen who had come homesteading west of Winnipeg in the
> early days of the century. Whenever they came to Winnipeg they
> would be at our house and my Aunt Mary would prepare a feed
> of salt herring and boiled potatoes and, speaking only Gaelic,
> they would have a ball ... There were MacCormicks from Sìthean,
> MacDonalds from Calva, MacArthurs from Clachanach and, of
> course, my aunt and her brothers from Sligineach.

The school roll on Iona was falling steadily, an intimation of the population decline the new century would see. The School Board used the decrease from 82 to 60 children in the ten years up to 1902 as an excuse for even more delay on building an extension to the school. Improvements demanded by the Sanitary Inspector in 1892, to provide a water supply and proper drainage, had been carried out by 1901. The Board tried the tack of approaching the Inspector of Poor and the Parish of Glasgow for a share of the costs of a new classroom, on the grounds that boarded-out children from the city rendered it necessary, but without success. Work on alterations finally began, however, and the repaired school and schoolhouse reopened in November 1903.

Mr James Wood had begun as schoolmaster in January 1900, assisted by Iona-born infant mistress Jetta MacDonald, and inspectors' reports continued to rate the standards of teaching as very high. The School Log Book for 1907 notes that Winnie Wood, Jeannie MacNiven and John MacArthur had left to enter Oban High School. They would have been about 14, the age when pupils normally left altogether. Two years later, seven former pupils of Iona school were in secondary education, a good number for a small rural place of the day. When Mr Wood retired in 1918 he received two gifts made by Alex Ritchie, a large copper-framed mirror from the islanders and a brass tray specially presented by former pupils. He had clearly won their respect and gratitude.

Visitors kept up an interest in the school. A gift of a bookcase and books from tour-operator Thomas Cook was followed in 1904 by another bookcase from James Coates of the Paisley cotton firm, who made similar presentations to schools in Argyll. Later that year, the books accumulated from donors since the 1820s found their own home in the public library, handsomely built in Mull granite by Fletcher of Tobermory and funded by Andrew Carnegie. The same summer, two Glasgow ladies gave prizes for a children's flower-gathering competition. And the entire school marched from the village to the Machair, banners waving excitedly as usual, for the annual games and picnic provided by the Duke of Argyll.

Also in 1904, the Inspector noted that the average attendance was forty-nine and that many class hours had been lost through epidemics. Attendance tended to be erratic when children were needed at home for particular tasks, such as harvest work or wrack collecting or potato lifting, but the fear of contagious illness was certainly another major reason. In the years before the First World War, influenza, whooping cough and scarlet fever all figure in this regard in the school records and in 1919 an outbreak of diphtheria was virtually to close the school and claim the life of Elizabeth MacPhail, 9 years old. Those born on the island were as vulnerable as the children who had started life in the congested streets of the city. Dr MacKechnie, giving evidence to the Highlands and Islands Medical Service Committee in 1912, stated that although the Glasgow boarders were often prone to illness when they arrived, their general health very soon improved.

The year before a second doctor – a Dr MacKenzie – had been appointed to help cover the parish, but as both men lived in Bunessan they had considerable difficulty ensuring adequate care as far as the head of Loch Scridain, to the lighthouse families on Erraid and over an often stormy Sound to Iona. They had a pony and trap and a bicycle between them to cope with this scattered community and agreed that a motor car, but for the expense, would be of great use.

Dr MacKechnie's evidence to the 1912 committee mentioned that a nurse supplied by the Jubilee Institution assisted him over the whole parish and that a midwifery nurse was resident on Iona. The latter was provided by the Govan Training Home which trained nurses for rural and Highland areas where medical help might be sparse or financially out of the reach of poorer folk. Dr MacKechnie declared that he was very satisfied with the nurses, that the people liked them and that the Iona midwife would usually stay with the mother for a week, undertaking valuable domestic work as well as nursing if necessary.

It is very likely that the midwife was Anne Wood, wife of the schoolmaster. The presentation on his retirement was made to them both, reported in the *Oban Times* as owing to Mrs Wood's 'needful and valuable nursing service'. A granddaughter has confirmed that she was sent to Glasgow to train in midwifery and nursing, paid for by the Duchess of Argyll. The family story is that soon after coming to Iona she had been much moved by the death of a mother and baby and wanted to give practical help. Duchess Ina, wife of the eighth Duke, was indeed an active patron of the Argyll District Nursing Association and Mrs Wood may have been able to appeal to her because of her own links with the Campbell family. She had once been companion to a maid-in-waiting of Princess Louise, later wife of the ninth Duke. Mrs Wood was known, too, to have a great knowledge of herbal medicines, as a number of local women will also have had at that time.

A child delivered by the Govan-trained nurse on Iona in the early years of the twentieth century grew up in a place where the traditional ties of kinship and community remained strong. Willie MacDonald, born in 1902, once said of his parents' contemporaries that their attitude to life seemed to reflect a contentment with whatever they had, that everyone was happy, that they were like 'one big family'. This is not necessarily an idyllic view, for it is not to deny that drudgery and distress were also present nor that people must inevitably have disagreed and wrangled and fallen out from time to time. But compared to the generations of half a century before, the islanders did now possess greater economic security and a higher level of material comfort. There was no flood of locals outwards nor a major influx of newcomers. The memory of living in a stable, close-knit society is a quite credible one.

And there was plenty going on, to occupy and entertain the young. Willie remembered watching the hewers at work in the covered part of the cathedral cloisters, dressing stones for the restored nave windows. Another focus for childhood curiosity must have been the marble quarry, abuzz with activity since a Glasgow company leased it from the Duke of Argyll in 1907 and began satisfying the Edwardian demand for ornamental marble furnishings. A photograph in David Viner's detailed account of the quarry's history shows a small boy – and no doubt there were more – amid the men grouped round the huge crane which swung the green-veined white blocks on to the outcrop of rock which served as a rough jetty for the waiting puffer.

For children there were also the endless distractions of sea and shoreline. But an island always lives with the risks that the sea – even in benign mood – can bring, and the young too had their share of tragedy. Late on a July evening in 1908, two teenage boys and a girl drowned when their dinghy capsized, just off Eilean a' Charbaid, a stone's throw from the end of the village. Archibald MacArthur heard their cries from Clachanach but he was too late. The dead girl had been boarded out with his aunt, Mrs Benham, and it is said old Ann

Cameron asked earlier that day if Rosina had washed her hair. But the premonition, if such it was, went unheeded. One boy managed to swim ashore and another girl had a narrow escape, caught by the hair as she went down for the third time.

The boat belonged to Angus MacPhail and he broke it up the next day. Superstition and the sea are seldom far apart. Just over twenty years earlier, also making a deep mark on the small community, one of the MacDonald weaver families lost two young brothers when the boat they had borrowed from the schoolmaster, Mr Kirkpatrick, was swept away. He too destroyed what was left of it. The boys' sister, a nurse, was returning to the mainland and they had ferried her over to Fionnphort. She never crossed the Sound of Iona again but always left with the steamer.

Yet the islanders had to live with, and to some degree from, the sea. Crucial to the transport of goods, livestock and fish, not to mention visitors, was a proper, well-maintained landing place. In the Argyll and Bute District archives there is a bulky file marked 'Iona Boat Slip 1908-1912'. It is a saga that illustrates the islanders' persistence and initiative when an issue was of direct concern to their community and livelihoods.

Early in 1908, the minister Archibald MacMillan chaired a meeting on the island where plans were approved for a new boatslip. The slipway had first been built in 1850 as part of the relief work during the potato famine, and it was now felt to be in a dangerous state. At low tide it had to be lengthened by two wooden gangways belonging to MacBrayne's but even this was insufficient at times and provided insecure footing for passengers ferried to and from the steamer. Quintin Bell of the Clyde Trust had drawn up the plan at a cost of £170. A local guarantee fund included contributions of £20 from David MacBrayne, £7.10/- from Martin Orme (the cargo steamer operators), and £15 from each member of a committee responsible for the upkeep. This was composed of Angus MacPhail, Malcolm Ferguson, Archibald MacArthur, Neil MacNiven, John MacInnes, Alexander Ritchie and Dugald Maclean. The Duke of Argyll was prepared to make a free gift of the site and the committee decided to seek grant aid from the Congested Districts Board which had been set up in 1897 and part of whose remit was to assist public works such as roads, harbours and piers.

This was not, in fact, the islanders' first attempt to benefit from the new Board. As far back as 1898, they had made an application for precisely the same purpose, to improve the boatslip which they stated was 'of vital importance for the traffic of the island'. This was refused on the grounds that it was primarily for tourist traffic and not the Board's reponsibility. Two people had also enquired whether the Board would supply motor boats for fishermen but with no success. Undaunted, the 1908 committee wished to try again. 'Nothing has been done by the Congested Districts Board for this island' they stated reproachfully, 'and we hope that something will now be undertaken.'

However, it took two years before the formal application, under the West Highlands and Islands (Scotland) Works Act 1891, was finally submitted. The recommendation for a grant had to come from the County Council, who made clear that this could not be forthcoming if any condition was attached to any local subscription. MacBrayne's was equally clear that it would only contribute provided no dues would be charged for use of the slipway. Things remained at stalemate for more than a year.

The Council also raised the question of what would be done about a particularly obtrusive rock at the end of the present slip. To this Mr MacMillan replied briskly that 'on the advice of a practical man the promoters have decided to carry the slip out straight and incorporate the rock in the structure'.

Practical men had never been lacking when it came to the ingenious use, or even removal, of natural features. The Carraig Fhada, the long outcrop of rock jutting out parallel to the pier, bears to this day the metal rings and signs of infilling which rendered it serviceable as a rough landing-place over at least two centuries. A large boulder used to obstruct the approach into Port Rònain and sometime in the nineteenth century someone must have scraped it once too often. Action was taken. A boat was roped firmly to the rock at low water and when the tide had risen sufficiently, both boat and boulder were towed out of reach. It is still visible between Eilean a' Charbaid and the north end of the village.

The estimated cost of the longer slip of just under 90 yards, including 40 yards of coping, was to be £225 and towards the end of 1910 the Congested Districts Board agreed to grant 75 per cent of this. The local promoters agreed to guarantee the remainder, making up the now-abandoned MacBrayne contribution from their own. The story was not over, however, as the landing dues question was revived by MacBrayne's who wrote in strong terms to the Board of Trade. Although its assertion that the boatslip was a public right of way in use 'from time immemorial' was a clear exaggeration, the company had spent effort and money on repairs over the years and any increased burden on its passenger fares was an understandable fear. It lodged a formal objection to landing rates late in 1911, as did Martin Orme and the Iona Cathedral Trustees.

The local committee then weighed in with their concerns. It would mean a higher cost of living for the crofters and fishermen plus the need for a policeman stationed on the island, which would be 'repugnant' to native and visitor alike, and their proposal was to lease the slip themselves at a nominal rent. Failing this, added Mr MacMillan tartly, 'they are prepared to take the work in hand themselves and be done with all boards and councils'. Irritation with bureaucracy is clearly not a modern phenomenon.

In effect, this is what they did. After further exchanges between the island and David MacBrayne, the steamer company agreed to undertake reconstruction of the slip with the help of local subscriptions. The a pplications to the Council and Congested Districts Board were withdrawn and work began in the spring of 1913. No dues were to be charged. The boatslip trustees were a company representative from MacBrayne's, the postmaster and the minister and this arrangement remained in place until ownership of the pier was transferred to Argyll County Council in 1955.

One detail was overlooked in the lengthy saga, however, although not by the meticulous Mr MacMillan. His final letter to the Council asked which plan had been forwarded to MacBrayne. This turned out to be the original, and not the amended one, which explained why the offending rock still lay off the end of the jetty. It was finally incorporated into the Council enlargements to the pier in 1956, nearly fifty years after 'a practical man' had made just that suggestion.

MacBrayne's close involvement in the boatslip question highlights the continued growth of visitor traffic to Iona. Paradoxically, one of the delaying factors had been a requirement to clarify the local population's need for the improvement since, as had been the problem in 1898, the government grant could not be given to help tourist traffic. This may have been a tricky point to argue, since the local economy was undoubtedly tied closely into the seasonal influx of visitors.

Kenneth MacKenzie, successor to the Ritchies at the Columba Hotel, gained permission from the estate for the addition of a north wing in 1907, owing to increased pressure on accommodation. That October, the *Oban Times* reported that house letting on the island had been 'very satisfactory' and that the Columba with its extra rooms had had 'a splendid season'.

At the individual croft level this was obvious too, as the demand grew from entire families wanting to take a house for one or two months in the summer. About 1904 Archibald MacArthur and his father began converting Clachanach to two storeys, with three upstairs bedrooms, two small bedrooms downstairs plus a scullery and sitting-room. The first summer-let was to Sir Donald MacAlister, principal of Glasgow University and one of the Iona Cathedral Trustees, while the family decamped to the adjoining barn.

In 1911, shortly after Archibald's marriage, he began to build a smaller house for his family's own use, with the help of John MacCallum – a Kentra stonemason. They obtained a redundant supply of excellent wood, for the internal partitions, from the Glasgow International Exhibition that year. The first son Dugald had been born in 1910, followed by Mary Katherine the next year and Neil Niven was to be born in 1914. The old custom of naming children after paternal and maternal grandparents in turn was still followed in the Clachanach family.

A second house or an extension became common on Iona over the next couple of decades and questions about the status of these were occasionally raised at hearings of the Land Court, which was created in 1912 to carry on some functions of the former Crofters Commission. The Small Landholders (Scotland) Bill of 1911 contained a provision requiring the landlord's consent for the erection of an extra dwelling-house, which would also need a special site value. Several cases had arisen in Arran, another island where summer-letting had early been established as a useful source of extra income. Discussing a dispute there in 1925, where a tenant had to remove a summer house, an *Oban Times* editorial expressed concern that the loss of letting revenue was not taken into account by the Land Court in awarding compensation. Nothing so contentious happened on Iona, however. In 1917, the Land Court agreed to treat the double house at Traighmòr as one since the two buildings were linked internally. This occasioned the invitation by Donald Cameron, delivered with enigmatic solemnity, that if the Court cared to make a site visit he would be pleased to show them the door.

The work on the bigger house at Clachanach in 1904 caused a minor stir in antiquarian circles when, just behind it, were unearthed the bones of a horse. These lay at a depth of 7 feet, under a kind of roofing formed of roughly squared granite blocks unlike the small round stones in the immediate vicinity. They seemed to have been deliberately laid over the animal's remains. Most of the bones were too fragile to survive exposure to the air but several teeth remained intact and were said to be those of a small horse of great age.

Did this apparently careful burial indicate a special and important animal? The Revd Archibald MacMillan's book on Iona, published in 1898, indicates a possible site for Columba's cell near to Clachanach. This had been earlier postulated by W. F. Skene in volume II of his *Celtic Scotland* (1877), and although the theory was to be overruled by later archaeological investigations, these were widely known books at the time. Thus the saint's white horse, the faithful servant described by Adomnán, was obviously a leading candidate and the newspaper columns buzzed briefly with speculation. Perhaps, on the other hand, it was once a faithful and favourite servant on the croft and had simply been given a special resting-place to please some MacArthur children of an earlier generation.

Dugald MacArthur died in 1909 aged 77. His daughter Helen, who was to have a distinguished nursing career, came home to care for him in his last months. In December of the previous year the Church of Scotland congregation presented him with a Gaelic pulpit Bible and black marble clock, whose inscription records that it was for 'faithful service in leading the praise in the parish of Iona for upwards of fifty years'. He had seldom been absent from the precentor's chair over the preceding half century. The Church, and its traditional form of worship, had been central to his life. Indeed, he had resisted the introduction of hymns, maintaining steadfastly that the psalms of David had long been good enough for him.

10

The Lads who will Never Return

On 8 August 1914 the *Oban Times* editorial began: 'Almost the whole of Europe is now in the throes of a struggle such as history has never before seen.' A huge crowd had gathered to see men of the Argyll and Sutherland Highlanders leave with the mid-day train, and a week later the Ross of Mull correspondent reported the departure of several young men to join the Scottish Horse, adding: 'The greatest enthusiasm prevails in the district.'

The Scottish Horse had been set up by Lord Lovat during the Boer War and the horse was requisitioned along with the recruit. A photograph has survived of this happening at Bunessan in the Ross of Mull, probably in 1914. The number and ages of all agricultural horses had to be registered with the army, in case they were required in time of war, but there is no recollection of either animals or Scottish Horse soldiers being mobilised from Iona itself. Several island men joined the Argyll and Sutherland Highlanders or the Highland Light Infantry while others went to sea, to the Royal Naval Reserve. The Mull and Iona Association in Glasgow published a Roll of Honour in April 1915, listing the men from the two islands on active service. Fifteen were from an Iona family. When completed, the total roll contained the names of over 300 officers and men.

Dugald MacArthur was not yet 5 years old when the war broke out. His first memory of it was an October Sunday morning in 1914 when his father called him outside. Behind Staffa, some six miles to the north, a line of grey battle ships was heading for the mouth of Loch na Keal while a detachment of cruisers swept steadily up from beyond Eilean Annraidh to follow them into shelter. It was the Grand Fleet. Archibald rowed the family over to Fidden on Mull that day to visit their MacNiven relatives, but Duncan MacColl, the farmhand left behind, spent the day spotting ships. On the others' return he told them he had counted fifty-seven.

The fleet spent three or four days in the safety of the loch, on the way from Scapa Flow to the reserve port at Loch Swilley in the north of Ireland. There had been a submarine alert, which was to be a fairly regular occurrence as the Germans ventured much closer inshore than they were to do in the Second World War. Navy activity was therefore not uncommon in Hebridean waters. Again, Dugald MacArthur has a vivid recollection from about 1917:

> I remember playing down by the shore when two Royal Navy destroyers came through the Sound from the north and one hit a sandbank straight on. The other slewed off, tried to pass a rope and eventually got it off. They did an about-turn and went back north, round the back of the island. Angus MacPhail came out in his dinghy and gave them hell – told them to look at their charts!

By October 1914 the whole of Argyll was a prohibited area, so that anyone passing in or out of the area needed a pass. The *Grenadier* stopped her summer sailings early in the war and was used for mine-sweeping but there was remarkably little disruption to cargo and year-round passenger shipping on the west coast. Latterly, smaller ships such as the *Hesperus* lighthouse vessel were escorted, and the *Dunara Castle* and *Hebrides* had a gun placed aft, plus a naval gun's crew on board. About 1917 the *Dunara* was painted with her 'coat of many colours', a camouflage of irregular blues and greys. It made her shape hard to distinguish against choppy waves and cloudy sky and submarines could not accurately judge her speed.

On Iona, Johnnie Campbell, an East End crofter, was named lookout by Seton Gordon who was officially responsible for these appointments in the Western Isles. A flag and telescope were taken to Cnoc an t-Suidhe, a small hill on the north shore. John MacInnes at Greenbank, towards the south end of the island, was made Head Coastwatcher. The 1st Argyllshire Volunteer Regiment was set up on the island and

Donald Black, who had been a sergeant in the Territorials in Edinburgh as a young man before coming home to Clachancorrach croft, was the obvious one to be in charge. He had also gone on to Bisley in Surrey as a crack shot. The Sergeant, as he was always known locally, put the men through their drills in the school playground.

At Clachanach, Dugald MacArthur learned to do a draw-through on the rifle issued to his father, to keep it clean, and remembers the practice pouch of five dummy bullets. The men trained in their ordinary clothes, perhaps with puttees round their boots, and only received uniforms quite late in the war. Dugald also recalls his father being away all day for an inspection at Knock Farm in Mull, early in 1918. A boat was sent from Salen to bring the Iona and Bunessan Volunteers round and their efforts were rewarded by a commendation from the Commanding Officer.

Alongside these unusual activities, much of the ordinary daily work went on as before for the islanders. Food supplies were not unduly affected, apart from restrictions on items such as sugar, as people could still rely on their own potatoes, eggs, fish and some mutton. A lot of pigs were exported to Glasgow, bringing in a little cash; horses continued to be sold at the Salen fair and stirks at the Bunessan market. One source of extra income, labouring at the marble quarry, came to an abrupt end with the cessation of the Iona Marble Company's operations. Some of the workforce will have left to join up and the company's lucrative trade with Belgium was cut off, leading to the company's liquidation by the end of the war. On the other hand, there were occasional bonuses, as when a box of lard or barrel of oil was recovered, left floating from a sunken ship. These fetched a pound of salvage money each. Dugald MacArthur once earned five shillings from Hector Maclean by alerting him to a barrel washed up on the shoreline.

An industry familiar of old, kelp-burning, made a brief comeback. The Board of Agriculture considered that kelp might revive in value since the import of substitute sources was again cut off by war, and it distributed a leaflet giving practical advice, particularly to the north and the outer isles. On Iona, fisherman Charles Kirkpatrick took up kelp-making in 1915 for a short while. In preparation for burning he piled the weed in long heaps along the Machair shore, where outlines of the kilns used a century before could yet be traced. Philip Tibbitt, who had been brought up on the island, continued the practice for a year or so after the end of the war, sending ten or fifteen sacks away at a time by cargo steamer.

The *Oban Times* occasionally printed letters received by relatives from men at the front. A moving one from Archibald MacPherson of Bunessan, a piper with the Scots Guards, conveys the weariness felt as early as January 1915 and the fellow feeling which emerged, even across army lines. On Christmas Day they had talked with the Germans and an officer had given him a souvenir of a coat button, saying he hoped it would all be over in six months. The letter went on: 'I think the Germans are tired of it … many of them were very nice fellows and did not show any hatred which makes me think they are forced to fight. I wrote you a letter telling you we made a bayonet attack. We lost a few men. The Germans helped us to bury them on Christmas Day.'

The previous month, Lachlan Maclean had written to his sister in Iona describing his work as Quarter Master Sergeant and telling her not to worry as his 'proverbial luck' would surely pull him through. Despite the hardship of three-week stretches in the trenches he added: 'We are getting looked after like lords thanks to the people at home and we all appreciate it.' The war effort at home was rapidly in full swing. Soon after hostilities were declared, the Ladies Guild of the Mull and Iona Association in Glasgow formed a work party in support of the Argyll and Sutherland Highlanders. On Iona itself a War Work Party met weekly during winter in the Argyll Hotel, a stalwart member from the very start being Mrs James MacArthur Sligineach who was no less than 93 when the war broke out.

By the end of 1916 the work party had sent off 365 pairs of socks and the next year the island branch of the YWCA made its own contribution of 103 knitted items for the Red Cross. There were flag days in aid of the Red Cross and concerts too, at one of which the participants included Sir Fitzroy Maclean of Duart and a daughter of Marjorie Kennedy Fraser. The National Egg Collection for the Wounded had a depot in Oban and it reported at the end of the war that Maggie MacNiven Iona had contributed a total of 522 eggs. Georgina MacMillan, the minister's wife on Iona, organised the cleaning of spaghnum moss to go to the Argyll Gathering Hall in Oban, the collection point for the whole district. In May 1918 Mr Munro MacKenzie

of Calgary appealed through the *Oban Times* that this effort should not
let up, as cotton wool for wound dressings was more and more difficult
to obtain. And he added, a trifle pointedly: 'Men need not think it is just
women's work; they can do a lot of cleaning spaghnum moss when
smoking their pipes of an evening.'

Visitors had continued to come throughout the war, both to the
hotels and houses for let, although in reduced numbers in the early
years at least. There are only fourteen names in the St Columba Hotel
visitors' book for 1915 although nearly twice as many appear the
following year. Daily passenger sailings had stopped but some may
have taken the *Dunara Castle* direct from Glasgow and others come
through Mull. In 1916 MacPhee of Aros was advertising the 'Overland
route to Iona', costing 25/- return for a seat in a motor car from Salen
Pier on arrival of the mail steamer twice a week. By 1918 this new tour
was reported to be very popular, bringing increased business to the
Iona ferryman.

A number of the regular visitors, whom the locals had come to know
well, were themselves on service or became involved in war-related
activities while on holiday. It was Mrs Pettigrew and her daughter, who
had been coming to Iona since 1898, who supplied wool for the
knitting party and they also endowed a bed, named the 'Iona Bed', in
No. 11 Scottish Red Cross Hospital in France where Miss Pettigrew
was on nursing service. Mr F. Stuart Silver, on sick leave from France,
gave a talk in the schoolhouse about his army work with the YMCA and
a Miss Neilson funded trips in Captain Maclean's motor boat for
convalescing soldiers and war workers.

Dr Dewar from Dunblane made perhaps the most unusual gift. He
arranged for a Reuters' telegram to be sent to Iona Post Office each
day, with the news from the front. It was common for the children to
scamper down after school to read it and run home with the latest
bulletin. Dugald MacArthur remembers the excitement, as 1918 wore
on, when it became clear that the German army was being gradually
pushed back. Then, on 11 November, the telegram arrived earlier than
usual. School was closed for the day and Coll MacDonald went to ring
the cathedral bell, echoing the peals of thanksgiving throughout the
land.

The men whose luck had held, like Lachlan Maclean from the

merchant's family, came home. Donald McVean, a grandson of the former Free Church minister, was later to relate to an annual gathering of the Mull and Iona Association that the end of the war found him in the Middle East and that he did what no one surely had done before – 'travelled on a free pass from Babylon to Iona'. Duncan MacColl, the Mull lad who had spent his day off watching the Grand Fleet slip into Loch na Keal in 1914, had been eager to join up as soon as he was old enough. About two years later he was away, coming back on leave to visit Clachanach in his Argylls' kilt at least once. But he was killed in March 1918 in the last major German offensive.

Energetic efforts began almost at once, on both sides of the Sound of Iona, to fund-raise for a War Memorial. There were concerts, often held in the open air in the school playground. At one held inside the school, in 1919, over £22 was raised from a song recital by Marjorie and Patuffa Kennedy Fraser, and the programme – specially painted by artist John Duncan – was even auctioned.

The islanders' first choice for a site for the War Memorial was the hillock within the Reilig Odhráin and the cathedral trustees gave their permission. The rocky foundation may have proved unsuitable, however, and the tall granite cross was finally unveiled in July 1921 just north of Martyrs Bay. The Revd Coll A. MacDonald, whose brother Hugh was listed among the dead, conducted the ceremony. Alex Ritchie talked of the impressive scenes on this spot in centuries past, when the bodies of Highland chiefs were landed there for burial. After Mr Wood paid tribute to the boys he had taught in school, there were few dry eyes among the company. The memorial bears eleven names, described as 'sons and grandsons of Iona' since several of them were from families who had already moved or emigrated. Two MacFarlane brothers from Bishop's Walk were lost at sea but Dugald and William Black, both privates in the Seaforth Highlanders Canada, had probably never set foot in Iona. Their father Alexander had left Clachancorrach before the turn of the century, but the wish that his sons, and others, be remembered in the community from which they stemmed was entirely fitting.

Across the water the memorial to those gone from the Creich part of the parish was unveiled in April 1920. It stands close by the present hall – then the school – and Mr Yuille, for many years schoolmaster there, gave the address. Janet Faulds, born in 1904 the youngest daughter of ferryman Coll Maclean, told the author in 1994 that that event was still clear in her mind's eye, its emotion undimmed by the years: 'I remember that perfectly well. It was sad, I remember my mother crying quite openly with the sadness, you know ... the boys that were killed. And the lovely singing they had and Mrs Yuille unveiling it. I remember that day plain as anything but I was upset at my mother crying.'

Janet's mother was a MacCormick, a sister of John of the Iona Press. Another brother, Donald, composed a pipe tune at the end of the war and called it 'The Lads who will Never Return'. These island communities still had their roots in a society used to seeing their menfolk go off to fight. Across a tiny bridge not two miles from the Creich War Memorial, and leading from a strath where a mere handful of ruined cottages dot the moorland today, they say that nineteen young men once marched to some war. Theirs was a long and honourable military tradition which they shared with corners of the Gaidhealtachd everywhere. And, as in so many other places, those who were left tended to look back on the First World War as a time when everything changed, when so much had been sacrificed that the same could never be given again. With the lads, many felt, had gone some aspects of the old ways and the old loyalties, and these too would never now return to the Ross of Mull and Iona.

11

Living from Land and Sea

In the course of a constituency tour in the late summer of 1919, Sir William Sutherland MP for Argyll addressed an open-air meeting near Iona jetty. As elsewhere, the newspaper report ran, the main questions concerned transport and land settlement. A committee had been set up in 1915 by the Board of Agriculture and Fisheries to prepare for the provision of smallholdings to men who had volunteered for the war. This was based on a desire to stem further decline in the rural population and so protect future food supplies. Impatience with the slow pace at which these promises were being fulfilled brought some ex-servicemen into direct conflict with landlords in the immediate post-war years, and again there were land raids, in Raasay, Lewis, North Uist and elsewhere.

In the Ross of Mull, the Duke of Argyll agreed that the Board take Ardfenaig farm, Eorabus on the Ardtun peninsula, and Cnocvuligan for division into crofts and this had gone ahead in 1915. On neighbouring Tiree, he offered Balephetrish farm but arguments over compensation for the tenant led to delay which in turn boiled over into a land grab by eight cottars in 1918. They were sentenced to ten days in prison by Oban Sheriff Court for their temerity.

On Iona there was no similar pressure for extra land. With the exception of Calva and Sandbank, where the people had gone to Canada, each croft was occupied by the same family whose case had been argued for them by Malcolm Ferguson at the Napier Commission nearly forty years before. The days of subdividing holdings had long gone; now one son stayed on the land and any brothers went to sea, emigrated or settled on the mainland.

Transport, however, did remain a live issue for the islanders as the efforts over the boatslip had demonstrated. Agitation was renewed in 1919 with a long petition to the County Council – to whom the Duke of Argyll had transferred ferry rights in 1910 – arguing that dependence on a ferry link by sail was now 'many years behind the times' and led to isolation for as long as a week in adverse weather conditions. A motor boat would be more reliable, to bring the doctor across in emergencies and hasten delivery of the greater number of perishable goods coming by post across Mull, now that the cargo steamer from Glasgow ran every ten days instead of weekly. The thrice-weekly mail service to Oban, by vessels such as the SS *Dirk*, had also stopped. It was to be a few years more, in the mid-1920s, before ferryman Coll Maclean acquired a motor boat – after his older son Alan returned from sea to operate it. Coll preferred to stay under the dipping lugsail of his 18-foot skiff which had already tacked back and forth across the Sound, fickle winds permitting, for nearly half a century.

In September 1919 the *Oban Times* carried a report from the West Highland Reconstruction Committee, of which there was a sub-committee for Bunessan and Iona district, recommending the extension of steamer services between Glasgow and Oban and the improvement of piers and fishing. It also considered there might be potential for government works in the Ross of Mull granite quarries, now silent for a decade, and in reviving the use of Iona marble as a cottage industry. Neither proposal made any progress.

Some trades and crafts carried on into the post-war years, although fewer than a generation earlier. The services of a wheel-turner, shoemaker or tailor were no longer needed, although knitting and sewing will have continued at the domestic level. Henrietta MacInnes from Greenbank, for example, who died in 1916, had been a skilled seamstress and regularly made clothes for other families in addition to her own. As the last of the old thatched cottages were replaced by improved single- or two-storey houses, joinery and building work remained in demand. John MacCormick, who trained as a joiner in Barrhead, was one islander who came back in the early 1920s to ply his craft at home. Angie MacKay also returned towards the end of that decade after serving as a boat-builder's apprentice.

There was still one weaving family in the village. Willie MacDonald was taught at first by his father Coll, working the pedals of the large wooden loom which they had brought in through the window of Tigh nam Beart and reassembled inside. Later Willie went out to Harris to learn the modern Hattersley loom, the kind he was to use himself.

MacKillop, the Bunessan blacksmith, came over once a month to the main Iona smiddy at the head of the jetty. Peter MacInnes, who died in 1895, had been the last local smith to work there regularly, although John MacInnes – known always as John Mòr – had served his apprenticeship with the blacksmith at Salen in Mull and operated a smiddy below Sandbank until the 1930s. Archibald MacArthur also had a small smiddy behind Clachanach, sufficient to sharpen tools or replace a horse-shoe lost on the hill. Angie Mackay was sent up there one day to help Malcolm Ferguson, or Calum Bàn to use his nickname, who had come over to mend a plough sock at the forge. The occasion was

Figure 6   Duncan MacGillivray, at the horse's head, and others at the door of the village smiddy, 1930s. Photograph courtesy of Elizabeth McFadzean whose parents spent their honeymoon on Iona in 1910; the family has visited regularly ever since.

memorable for the spectacular explosion of oaths when Calum opened
his tool bag and was instantly enveloped up to his white hair in a
swirling white cloud. His wife, Betsy, must have plucked a hen – 'Oh,
Calum was swearing and it was him who could swear ... you couldn't
see him for feathers!'

The village smiddy served also as storehouse for goods coming and
going by cargo steamer every ten days. Animal feed, grass seed and
groceries were ordered in bulk from Glasgow firms such as
MacFarlane Shearer, Smith & MacKay and Hamiltons. Some trade
went the other way, for example the eggs sent regularly to Hamiltons
by Janet MacArthur at Clachanach, in exchange for credit on her next
order.

In addition, local business was brisk enough to maintain three shops
on the island during the first decades of this century. Mary Ann
Maclean took over the running of the family general store after her
mother died in 1914. As would be expected, the Post Office sold postcards and souvenirs, in particular the fashionable white china made by
Goss and embellished with 'Iona' or the Argyll crest. But between the
wars it also stocked a certain amount of groceries, meat, bread and
some hardware items.

The most entrepreneurial establishment, perhaps, is still remembered as 'Martha's shop'. In 1914, Martha MacInnes of Greenbank
croft married master mariner Malcolm Macleod from Bernera in
Harris. He spent long spells at sea and Martha opened a small shop in
a room of Staffa Cottage where they lived. About 1922 the family
moved along the village street to Roseneath and built a hut to house
the shop, just above the beach. The visitors who rented holiday houses
boosted trade considerably, often sending large orders in advance, and
Martha's daughter May recalls her mother's ability to anticipate their
every demand and the exotic goods that would herald the summer season: 'sandshoes and sunhats hung beside branches of bananas still on
their stalks and the counter was piled high with confectionery of all
kinds'. Martha's brother John Mòr supplied mutton which she would
cut up herself, selling the front pieces at a shilling a pound and the
prized back legs at one and six. There were the big round cheeses from
Coll and the large floury loaves delivered by the *Dunara* and carried
home in snowy-white pillow cases, several at a time, to last until the
steamer next called.

Figure 7 Unloading coal from the puffer at Martyrs Bay. Photographed by Donald B. MacCulloch, c.1925.

Nearly every household still fished for the table, or benefited from a neighbour's catch. Visitors followed the custom too; after the excitement of a fishing expedition, Sheila Russell remembered her brothers trotting along the village street proudly carrying a string of fish, all gratefully received. Their generosity only backfired once, when they had left a couple of glistening mackerel in George Ritchie's hut, unaware that he had just taken off on one of his periodic voyages. When Dugald MacArthur ran on an errand to Hector Maclean's at Sligineach he seldom returned without a couple of flounders, sun-dried on the wall. The two Hectors, Maclean and MacNiven, were particularly skilled at setting lines on the sandy bottom of the Sound which was famed for the flat fish. In August 1918 the local contributor to the *Oban Times* wrote of 'the unrivalled reputation of the Iona flounders' and of recent catches exceptional in quality and quantity. It was not long after the end of the war that Donald MacColl, nicknamed somewhat appropriately 'the Sgadan' – 'the herring' – made a famous haul of 1,000 saithe in a single evening off the island's west coast.

So the sea still provided a plentiful harvest and made a significant contribution to the year-round diet but, as in preceding generations, no one turned entirely to it from the land. Charles Kirkpatrick in the village was the only full-time fisherman, concentrating on lobsters which he packed with seaweed into wooden boxes to go once a week by the *Dunara* to Glasgow and Billingsgate. His usual return was half a crown per lobster.

Agricultural output declined throughout the country during the depressed years of the 1920s and early 1930s. Although the situation in Argyll was generally better than in the north and in the Outer Isles, abnormally wet winters in 1923 and 1924 did lead to widespread failure in grain and potato crops. The Board of Agriculture offered to provide seed oats and seed potatoes at six shillings per hundredweight, half the usual price, and those unable to afford even this could obtain a credit slip in lieu of cash from a Local Distress Relief Committee. Crofters' meetings in Bunessan and Creich in February 1924 agreed to apply to the Board for this assistance. The bigger holdings in Iona may have lessened the impact of these poor seasons, but the general drop in livestock prices during the 1920s is bound to have affected incomes there, as everywhere.

There was the occasional bonus, for example when Archibald MacArthur sold a pig at the Glasgow market for the unprecedented sum of £24, nearly twice the usual price. He took some care over his pigs, arousing much local interest by his patent device of setting wooden blocks into the wall of the pighouse, with battens against which the sow could lie and so avoid squashing her piglets. By now they were largely for home consumption, however, providing home-cured ham, bacon and 'maragan' (black pudding), while cattle, sheep and horses remained the principal exports.

Crofting communities have long been characterised by the multifarious nature of their economic base. In other words, most crofters have always done a little bit of this and a little bit of that and here was no exception. Archibald MacArthur had several additional occupations. From his father he had taken over two responsibilities, that of gravelling the island's public road and that of acting as agent for the cargo company, now MacCallum Orme, landing and loading goods from the steamer. For this he had to buy and maintain his own vessels and in 1931 he ordered a new 22-foot boat from MacQueen of Easdale with a two-cylinder Kelvin engine. This towed the sturdy 'sgoth mhòr' (big skiff) with its 20-foot lugsail which had served for many years.

Archibald needed a dinghy too for regular trips to Mull where he sold policies for the Prudential Insurance Company. Although boats went back and forth all day, his dog Jack, watching from the house on Iona, always knew which was his master's leaving Fionnphort and trotted down to the shore to meet him. For a few years before the First World War, Archibald also had a spell as postman, something which Archie MacDonald had good reason to remember. As small boys are wont to do he had kept asking if there was a parcel for him, and one day the postman brought one – a lamb! For years it was kept in the garden at the back of Lovedale, the MacDonalds' home in the village. The animal's eventual fate, once its status as a household pet was outgrown, is not recalled but no doubt one of the local shops benefited.

From the advent of the summer pleasure steamers, men were needed to row the passengers ashore, both at Iona and Staffa. For the *Grenadier*, from the close of the war, four crofters made up the crew – Donald Cameron Traighmòr, in charge, Hector Maclean Sligineach, Duncan MacArthur Achabhaich and Sandy MacDonald Machair.

Figure 8   The rowing crew, 1920s, with the *Grenadier* behind: (left to right) Willie MacDonald, Duncan MacArthur, Hector Maclean and Donald Cameron. Each is wearing an 'Iona Boatman' jersey, issued by MacBrayne. Photograph courtesy of Kath Cameron.

Two of them were at the oars of each 30-foot long red tender, while a sailor from the steamship came on board to steer. It was hard work to get a heavy load of up to fifty passengers underway, and on rough days the men might double up on the oars of a single boat. Often, to save time, one red boat would then be towed by the steamer to Staffa where a skiff from Gometra was also on hand for the ferrying. Two masts were stowed under the seats of the tender and if wind and tide were favourable the Iona crew sailed back. Many times, however, it was a long row home and their few shillings overtime were well earned.

The tragic loss by fire of the *Grenadier* in the early hours of 6 September 1927 was a shock to islanders and regular visitors alike. Dugald and Neil MacArthur, in their school lodgings in Oban, were woken by the commotion and ran down to join a large crowd on the North Pier. Three crew members died, including the captain. The next season, the *Fusilier* took over the Iona and Staffa run and changes

Figure 9 Loading sheep into the *Dunara Castle*; includes (left to right) Dugald MacArthur, Jimmy Hay, Johnnie Dougall and, behind, Neil MacArthur. Photographed by Donald B. MacCulloch, *c.*1938.

followed too in the local employment of ferrymen. Her captain, considered less bold than Captain MacArthur of the *Grenadier*, anchored much farther out, and to save time MacBrayne hired retired sea-captain Archie Maclean to tow the rowing boats in and out with his motor boat. In 1929, this slightly cumbersome arrangement was soon replaced by a contract with John Mòr, who supplied his own motor boats for the Iona and Staffa landings up until the Second World War. The first boats provided by MacBrayne's shortly after the war were named, appropriately, the *Iona* and the *Staffa*.

Willie Coll, as Willie MacDonald was always known after the old style of linking a person's name to that of their father, had a long association with the red boats. He began at 17 in the rowing crew, replacing Sandy MacDonald in 1919, and continued until 1953. His father Coll supplemented his own income from weaving, and from his care-taker duties for the cathedral trustees, with earnings from an unusual sea-borne source. He made tubes for draining wounds from the stems of Laminaria, the coarse seaweed commonly known as tangle. Willie would help him carry bundles home on their backs from the Machair shore and hang them from a beam above the fireplace. Once the stems shrank a little, Coll would then work at them to get the smoothness he needed and put a thread through the finished tubes, a few inches long. Willie thought his father was the only one on the island to do this, and remembered him working every night at it for several years, to meet orders from a medical firm in Germany.

12

The Visitors

The most reliable little bit of extra income, however, available to the majority of households on Iona one way or another, came from visitors. During the inter-war decades the numbers seeking long summer-lets steadily grew, and the £25 or £30 per month went a considerable way to help maintain the houses all year and cushion the impact of lower prices for lambs and stirks. Those spending time on the island patronised the local shops, bought eggs, milk or potatoes from crofters, and hired boats for picnics and fishing expeditions. Receipts kept by David Russell, for example, who took his family to Iona each year from the late 1920s, show that on average he paid Hector MacNiven at Maol 3d. a pint for milk, 2/- for a dozen eggs and 3/- for carting luggage. One summer he settled a bill of £5.4/- from John MacInnes for a number of boat trips.

In June 1928, Miss Christine Hammer presented Janet MacArthur at Clachanach with a guest book and entered her name on the first page. She was a teacher from New York City who came as a boarder for several years and who also regularly took back Ritchie jewellery for sale in America. Who knows how many examples of Iona Celtic Art found a home across the Atlantic thanks to Miss Hammer's enthusiasm.

In addition to high-season lets, Clachanach was one of the first to provide full board for individuals in May, June and September. An extension was put on to the big house in 1924, making five bedrooms plus the innovation of an upstairs bathroom, the water piped from a tank on the lower slopes of Dùn I. A smoking-room was built at the end of the house, an idea somewhat ahead of its time but much appreciated by the guests.

Boarders still meant a lot of extra work of course. Jugs of hot water had to be taken upstairs each morning and hot wheaten scones made for breakfast. The rooms were cleaned every day, beds turned down, shoes polished. Wash-day at the well in the field below the house might be a chore of the past, but laundry baskets of sheets had to be sent away, towels and bedspreads washed and mangled by hand. At night there were lamps to light, the table to set, cruets to be refilled. By now there were three more in the MacArthur family – Catriona born in 1916, Eilidh in 1919 and Margaret in 1921. As soon as the girls were old enough, they did their share of helping. There were always one or two maids, often from the Outer Isles, and along with at least one farmhand the total to be fed three times a day could be as many as twenty-five.

The boarders paid £3 a week and they received three full meals a day plus afternoon tea, and a jug of milk and biscuits were left out for anyone returning from an evening stroll. Janet would take bookings only from week to week – requests to stay for ten days, for example, would be politely turned down – so that the beds were full the whole summer. It was a shorter season than nowadays and this was the only way it would pay. At other houses which began to take boarders, Traighmòr and Cùlbhuirg for example, the story was the same: it was a lot of work, but the visitors were given plenty of good wholesome food and a hospitable welcome.

The 'regulars' became thoroughly established during this period, some already in their second generation. It was customary for the houses not to take bookings, whether for lets or boarders, before 1 January of any year. By the second or third, a stack of letters had arrived, many guests hoping for a return visit. 'We knew them all' is the simplest and most commonly repeated reference to holiday-makers when those who grew up on Iona between the wars look back to those days. People identified with the place where they most commonly stayed. Eilidh and Margaret MacArthur organised 'Clachanach against the World' hockey matches, and the regular guests held winter reunions, to which Dugald and Catriona were invited when they were studying in Glasgow. And when Eilidh went to gym college in

Dunfermline, her fellow students were amazed at the number of weekend invitations she received from Edinburgh regulars.

It was impossible for visitors not to be aware of, and not take some part in, ordinary island life and recollections remain warm and vivid to this day. Carrie Kain, whose parents took Lagandorain every July and August from 1922, remembers the everyday tasks – Flora Campbell churning butter, her daughter Maggie hanging up fish to dry or laying carrageen seaweed (used for milk puddings) out on the grass. And as children they would lend a hand with whatever was happening, hay-making, herding, milking or fishing for mackerel off rocks at the North End. Carrie's husband Eric Robertson went to Sandbank with his family from 1929 and he was one of many visiting youngsters who eagerly took to the ocean waves for much of their holiday, in this case in John Mòr's boat.

Isobel Day was a young nanny in Edinburgh in 1926 when her employers, the Jamiesons, started going to Traigh Bàn for six weeks each year. She learned to feel flounders under her toes as the tide ebbed over the sands and, sometimes, to catch them. The MacDonalds at Ardionra would bring the family crabs from the rock pools and take them out fishing when the time was right for mackerel, delicious fried in oatmeal. On walks with her small charge, Menie, she came to recognise many of the islanders and other visitors, and vice versa. She recalled the kindness experienced when one year she contracted scarlet fever and had to remain behind, cared for by Mrs Jamieson and a doctor on holiday at one of the hotels, who checked her condition every day and refused any payment.

The decamping of an entire family to Iona, often complete with maid or nanny and for several weeks or months, was an undertaking in itself in those days. A large crate being slung off the *Dunara*, with the piano belonging to the Service family who took Traighmòr for many years, was an annual event. For the youngsters of the time these safaris across Scotland are often as clearly recalled as the holidays themselves. Harold Troup's parents had visited Iona before the First World War and they returned as a family from the 1920s. Their luggage consisted of thirty-two packages with green labels which had to be counted at Princes Street Station, Edinburgh and again at all points west, including on the two cars hired from the MacCallums to take them through Mull.

Flora Ewing's father John had been born and brought up on Erraid, where his father was principal lighthouse keeper and then captain of the lighthouse vessel. As a boy, John knew the Iona folk of his own generation, including Angus MacPhail, and it was a chance visit by Angus to their home in Edinburgh that prompted the Ewings to try the island for a holiday in 1924. They went for two months every year after that, and in 1939 bought Rose Cottage, at the end of the village street, building it up to two storeys and renaming it 'Erraid', echoing the old links with the lighthouse island.

There was great excitement for Flora and her sisters as the summer trek westwards drew near. A list of food was made up and provisions dispatched in tea chests by Coopers. About a week before departure, a porter from Newhaven Station collected their trunk, which travelled ahead of them to Oban. Then it was the overnight train from Princes Street Station, waking up to find Danny MacFarlane, Oban Porter No. 12, with his peaked cap and waxed moustache, ready to take the luggage on to the waiting steamer.

The visitors made significant contributions to the social as well as economic life of the island. Three concert reports in the *Oban Times* of 1929 hint at the appeal of these highly popular, occasionally even exotic, summer entertainments. The headline for one reads 'Sir Harold Boulton in Iona. A Famous Concert' and describes how the musician, who owned the island of Inchkenneth off Mull for a short period, presided over a 'super-excellent' evening during which his wife sang 'Fionnphort Ferry'. This was the song composed by Sir Harold in honour of Coll Maclean, who had just retired after over fifty years as Iona ferryman. A later concert included dancing by a guest at Maol farmhouse, a young Russian lady called Anna Varenska who had been taught ballet by Madame Pavlova herself. And in July, Marjorie Kennedy Fraser and her daughter Patuffa gave a song recital, one of their 'fascinating and world famous entertainments' which this time was for the more modest aim of helping furnish Iona's new hall.

No longer did concerts and dances have to be squeezed into the school or, in summer, into MacBrayne's boathouse. Opened to an enthusiastic crowd by Professor Cormack in July 1927, the Iona hall was built after four years of fund-raising efforts in which the visitors

Figure 10 Captain Archie Maclean, in oilskin coat, chatting to visitors at the door of his sister's shop. The board advertises his summer boat trips to nearby islands.

Figure 11 Visitors outside the St Columba Hotel, summer 1931. Photograph courtesy of Helen Goldie.

were as energetic as the islanders. It had a sprung floor, unusual for a village hall in those days, and it was completed free of debt. Treasurer Ian MacKenzie published details of the fund as it stood by August 1925, and a variety of concerts, whist drives and bazaars, plus donations from home and abroad had already totalled over £300.

Agreement on the site and the plans for the hall had run into the occasional mild squall in the course of local discussions, a state of affairs recorded for posterity in traditional fashion – satirical verse – by brothers Bob and Johnnie MacLelland. Johnnie had worked at Traighmòr as a boy and then moved to Clachanach where Bob joined him from Glasgow about 1920. A kenspeckle figure in later years on the red boats, Bob is remembered for his poems and paintings on local themes but especially for 'The Hall that was Built on the Top of Dun I', which was printed and sold in aid of the fund-raising. It pokes wry fun at some Iona characters, several of whom were themselves outstanding masters of the spoken word. Angus MacPhail was famed throughout the district as an eloquent and entertaining chairman, speech-maker and performer of his own witty songs. Other favourites included Duncan MacGillivray, Malcolm Ferguson, Alex and George Ritchie. It was Bob MacLelland too who kept many a dance going in the hall with his sparkling dulcimer-playing, often along with Lachie Cameron or Janet MacDonald on the melodeon. And there was always a piper.

In August 1929, Professor Cormack, along with that other unfailing summer visitor Mr G. W. Service, organised the children's sports at Traighmòr. This annual event, held alternately at the South or North End, was eagerly anticipated by the island's youngsters who always began the day with a march from the village, flags waving and excitement mounting. That September they also had a party in the hall, given by Lady Mary Glyn, a visitor to the Columba Hotel, and later there was the usual Hallowe'en treat with apples, oranges and wonderful decorations provided by the faithful Miss Pettigrew.

The effort to build the hall, however, had overtaken the usual fund-raising to run the adult games and regatta which had been revived annually since 1897, with a gap during the war years. The last Iona Games were in 1925. A Games day was planned for August 1926 but was rained off, much to the disappointment of Dugald MacArthur who had to go back to Oban High School without defending his hop, step and leap record. There were still the Tiroran Games, run by Brigadier General Cheape from 1922 until 1937 and immensely popular throughout the Mull area. Neil MacArthur, who was a very good athlete, competed there successfully several times as he did, too, at the Tobermory, Oban and Inveraray Games.

It is said that few islanders or fishermen ever used to be able to swim, although Archibald MacArthur was an exception. A good swimmer, he taught his daughters in the bay below Clachanach. Earlier, other Iona children had the chance to learn from a London stockbroker called Walters who came on holiday in the years before and after the First World War. He would balance them on their stomachs on the grassy hillocks above Martyrs Bay to practise the strokes. So for a few years, swimming competitions took place on Regatta day, although most of it was devoted to the keenly contested races for rowing, motor and sailing boats.

The fact that his father's boat with its one cylinder always came in last did not cloud Iain MacCormick's memory of the tremendous fun of these regattas. And they were by no means only fun for the boys, as the enthusiastic recollections of Annie Coll, a daughter of Coll MacDonald, testified. She rowed once with her sister Janet and Charlie MacPhail as cox, in a boat with a heavy centreboard which they did not like, but her father shouted encouragement from the smiddy corner. He had said not to worry about the weight, it would carry them along all the better once they got up speed and, sure enough, they won. Coll himself was the first to have an outboard engine, a Wisconsin from America, yet he still came only second in a race against the old inboard motor boats.

Folk came over from the Ross of Mull for the Regatta and even from as far as Tiree in the earlier years, and of course lots of visitors took part. Major D. B. Anderson from Cove, who presented a cup for one of the competitions, brought a sailing skiff with him on holiday specifically for the races, and one occasion that passed into local legend was when Parlan MacDonald from Cnocvuligan used shrewd seamanship to pip him at the post. Dugald MacArthur was there:

They must have gone up to Kentra first, then down the Sound and back to the village. The wind fell away and the ebb tide had begun and when they came round the black buoy for the last time, towards the village, Parlan went straight in to Traighmòr and crept along, skirting the rocks. You see he was avoiding the tide, while the others made a straight line to the village but then were stopped, were even going backwards ... while Parlan came right in, though he covered about twice the distance, and at Martyrs Bay, you know where the rock sticks out, he came right into the bay ... the wind was so light, he had his brother leaning the boat over on the leeward side ... then he went straight out and over the line. I remember Anderson was about fifty yards behind and he was clapping, everyone was clapping!

The first local report from Iona in the *Oban Times* of 1929 was about the Golf Club, which had met on 27 December to compete for the monthly medal. This was the MacLeod Medal, presented by an aunt of George MacLeod who came often on holiday. Former holder Ian MacKenzie retained it with a scratch score of eighty-one and Johnnie MacCormick was runner-up. On 1 January foursomes were held when Mary MacMillan and Calum Cameron came away with the top score, followed by Maggie MacPhail and Ian MacKenzie. This match was now a firm New Year's Day tradition, with most of the island in attendance and many of the men in kilts. Some who had played shinty in their youth took quickly to golf and became very good players. Others joined in for the fun of it once a year and went round the course with their one club. Clubs and bags could be stored at the MacMillans' house, beside the road to the Machair, and visitors made use of this too during the summer.

One category of visitors so numerous and colourful that they earned a particular place in the island's memory were the artists. Many travel books from the eighteenth century onward include sketches or engravings of Iona scenes and several well-known painters came there in the late nineteenth century. William McTaggart Senior was among these, for example, as was Sam Bough who on one occasion visited both Iona and Erraid with Robert Louis Stevenson, while Dhu Heartach lighthouse was under construction. The *North British Daily Mail*'s Iona correspondent reported in August 1877 that prominent among the visitors were 'a number of artists who are to be seen daily on every spot of interest, busily sketching the historical scenes of St Columba or the beautiful landscape scenery'.

Yet it is the stream of artists in the earlier part of the twentieth century who are best remembered. The East End folk were used to seeing them trooping past on a good day, haversacks and canvas strung over their shoulders, heading for favourite spots by the north shore. Near Traigh an t-Suidhe, one particular rock where they cleaned their brushes bore bright traces of paint for years. The island has qualities instantly apparent to the artist's eye. From it a range of landscape shapes are in view, providing perspective in the middle and far distance; its clear light, and the sandy shallows that fringe its coast, give its waters the translucent blue and green hues that have become almost synonymous with Iona.

Francis C. B. Cadell first fell under Iona's spell in 1912 and he returned again and again. A familiar figure in kilt and tammie, he was held in great affection by locals and many other regular visitors. He would let the children peer over his shoulder and test them on the colours in the sky. Also well liked was Samuel J. Peploe, who stayed on his early visits at Cùlbhuirg and later in the village. William Crawford combined his interests in painting and boat-designing by bringing fellow-artists such as Robert Burns and George Houston on cruises along the west coast. He had known Cadell too since student days and later they both had studios in Ainslie Place, Edinburgh. Crawford's wife, and her parents and grandmother before her, had gone to Iona on holiday and they eventually acquired the former granite quarriers' cottages at Tormore on the opposite side of the Sound as a painting and sailing retreat. The Iona people used to refer to the crane silhouetted on the skyline above the upper quarry as 'Crawford's easel'.

John MacGhie often stayed at Lagandorain and Penelope Beaton at Achabhaich where the barn also regularly housed a group of young artists known collectively as 'the barnsters'. James Shearer spent several seasons at Clachanach, preferring the simplicity and peace of a small room in the end of the old barn where meals were brought out to him. At his easel on the jetty one day, working on one of his delicate watercolours of the village street, Shearer was asked why he had not included the Bishop's House. 'Don't like it. I never put it in' was the straightforward reply. If such licence led to future confusion when attributing dates, it clearly did not unduly worry the artist!

William Mervyn Glass, whose vivid seascapes were later reproduced in a series of postcards, was some years in the old bothy by the Columba Hotel and other times in the wee house at Clachanach. Clearing up at the end of one summer, the MacArthur girls found several finished canvases casually tucked away under the eaves. And when Eilidh married, Glass asked her over to Ardionra where he was that year and presented her with a small picture, then worth three guineas. It was very common to receive or give a painting by one of the regular artists for weddings or other events.

Today, when huge sums are paid for a single work and thousands flock to prestigious exhibitions, it is easy to forget that these men were neither well-off nor ostentatious in their ways. Where a few of them have achieved widespread fame, this has followed some considerable time after their deaths. In the case of Cadell, for example, the people whom he met on Iona and who regularly purchased his work – in particular the Services, but also the Kains and the Russells – were a crucial source of support in his early career.

Two burials in the ancient Reilig Odhráin during 1929 reflected different sides to the strong pull of Iona for growing numbers of people. In August the ashes of Dr MacGregor, superintendent of the Victoria Infirmary in Glasgow, were brought to the island at his own express wish. It was the first time ashes were interred in the graveyard. He was one of the stalwart band of regulars, having come with his family for many years. The trustees were to give permission for several burials, for similar reasons, over the next few years. Indeed, in 1946 they were to consider the possibility that ground between the cathedral and the road be set aside for 'eminent personalities' who desired to be buried on Iona. But this did not ever transpire.

Another example was David Munro Fraser who died in 1931 while staying at Cnoc Mòr, the house he built on Iona in 1912 for holidays and retirement. He had been a noted Chief Inspector of Schools and a great enthusiast for the history and language of the Gael. He had the idea of instigating an open-air Gaelic service on Sunday afternoons, although only one such is recalled when he gathered a small congregation in the hollow above the Maol brae.

And in June 1932, a large crowd accompanied the ashes of Marjorie Kennedy Fraser aboard the *Lochfyne* from Oban. She had died two years earlier but a public appeal for a memorial, headed by Sir John Lorne MacLeod, claimed that 'the sacred isle was the only appropriate resting place for the Sweet Singer of the Hebrides'. Local people joined family and friends in the Reilig Odhráin for the interment beneath a carved stone designed by artist John Duncan. They included Alex Ritchie who had assisted with the memorial arrangements and Donald Cameron of Traighmòr, where Mrs Kennedy Fraser and her daughters had often holidayed. Lea McNally, a well-known street entertainer in Oban and on the steamers, was among those present, and the strains of 'The Road to the Isles' tinkled out on his dulcimer as the party dispersed.

In November 1929, however, the second funeral of a visitor that year was a more sombre affair. Norah Emily Fornario had been found in the hills south of Loch Staonaig, dead from exposure after being missing for two cold nights and days. She had been on Iona for several months, staying latterly with the Camerons at Traighmòr where she spent her time in the study of faith-healing, claiming to practise it telepathically by going into periodic trances. She was erratic in her habits, sometimes writing continuously through the night, and had once before precipitated a search party when she failed to return from a walk. Yet Miss Fornario did not impose her beliefs on the local people and is recalled as a pleasant woman in her mid-30s, tall and dark with the striking looks of her Italian ancestry.

Newspapers reported, wrongly, that she died on Sìthean hill, probably jumping to the conclusion that someone of her spiritualist leanings must be linked to the landmark where fairies were said to dance and St Columba had a vision of angels. The circumstances in which she was found were certainly strange. Her body was unclothed, although unharmed. She had a silver cross on a chain round her neck and a cross had been cut out of the turf, the knife discarded nearby. Whatever the mental or emotional disturbance that drove her out to the hills that night, the result was a human tragedy which touched the islanders.

In the absence of any immediate relatives, they laid her to rest in the Reilig Odhráin, among their own.

The work of the Iona Cathedral Trust to maintain the ecclesiastical remains continued to attract interest. In 1917, Mr J. J. Spencer and family approached the trustees offering to restore the ruined nunnery cloisters and lay out the garden in memory of their mother. MacGregor Chalmers was authorised to prepare plans but two years later there was a new proposal. The Spencers wished simply to see the nunnery preserved as it was and the grounds kept up with the help of a trained gardener. Over the years the capital sum they donated ensured that a riot of colour each spring and summer brought pleasure to local people and visitors alike. A newspaper article from 1936 evoked the beauty of the golden rod, sea campion, tall white marguerites and pink climbing roses which filled the old enclosed walls. And on the stone seats, like embroidered pew cushions, were mosaics of thyme, bugloss, yellow bedstraw and tiny purple pansies.

The garden was first laid out and looked after by a Miss Crawford, who lodged in the village for a few years. Later it passed into the care of Mrs Hannah MacCormick, wife of the local joiner, who also assisted the Ritchies in their shop. In the early 1930s a visitor from Glastonbury sent her three propagated cuttings from the town's famous Holy Thorn. They were planted in the shelter of the refectory wall but only one flourished for long, the others succumbing one severe winter. By the time Mrs MacCormick retired in the 1960s, the Spencer funds had also been depleted. Unfortunately, then, no one could give the same regular attention to the gardens and the Glastonbury thorn fell victim to a workman's spade during a periodic bout of tidying up.

The trustees had cause to be grateful also to D. Guthrie Dunn, a keen young yachtsman who had often visited the island with his father and who was aware of the cathedral tower's empty belfry. The whereabouts of only one of the medieval monastery's bells is known for certain; at some point after the Reformation it was removed and ended up in the Old Lowland Church, Campbeltown. Mr Dunn presented a handsome, twenty-two hundredweight bell which was dedicated at an impressive service in June 1931. Over five hundred came by special excursion steamer, the moderator the Revd Dr John Graham conducted worship and Dr Neil Ross gave an address in Gaelic. Sir Harold Boulton again sprang into verse with 'Iona Bells', a poem translated into Gaelic by Father John MacMillan of Barra. Tragically, Mr Dunn was drowned two years later, on the homeward stretch of a round-the-world cruise.

During the early 1920s Messrs Jardine and Grant from the Ministry of Works were employed on the island on behalf of the Iona Cathedral Trust. They undertook pointing and preservation work on the cathedral cloisters, St Oran's Chapel and the nunnery and they built up the walls of St Ronan's Church. No further restoration on a major scale was at that point in prospect. Yet it was inevitable that, once the cathedral choir and nave were returned to full use, speculation about the adjoining monastic buildings would soon follow.

13

Students and Schooldays

In the *Transactions of the Scottish Ecclesiological Society* of 1911 James Wilkie, BL FSA, quoted the prophecy that 'Iona shall be as it was' and hoped that cloisters, chapter-house and refectory would soon be as they were in Benedictine days. He also posed the question: 'What purpose is the reparation of Iona to serve?' His own reply was to echo a proposal put forward by the Revd Professor James Cooper, former moderator, in correspondence as early as 1903 and again in a sermon preached on the island in 1909. Professor Cooper felt that the Iona site would be eminently suitable as a seminary for young Highlanders intended for the ministry and, in summer, as a retreat for missionaries on furlough. It should be a centre of Celtic learning, to include Gaelic alongside the Latin and Greek required for university, and a training in Gaelic and English psalmody would bring the bonus of 'a delightful choir' for the cathedral services.

The cathedral trustees were to find the association of Iona with literature and learning a strongly recurring theme during the 1920s and 1930s. In 1923 they received notice of the will drawn up by Robert Lamont Ritchie, minister of Creich in Sutherland. Under its generous terms, a library was to be collected and set up within Iona Cathedral, specialising in the history of the Scottish and Irish Gaels, St Columba and the Scottish church in general. These books were to be made permanently available to islanders and visiting students. Robert Ritchie also requested that efforts be made to acquire the original manuscript of Adomnán's *Life of Columba*, which had been taken to the monastery of Schaffhausen in Switzerland for safekeeping centuries before. His brother George drew attention to this specific plea in a newspaper article in 1934, the year after Robert's death, but nothing further came of the idea. When Alex Ritchie died in 1941, he too left books on Celtic art and literature to the Cathedral Trust along with a small legacy for upkeep of the library. Today it is a pleasant, book-lined study, another lasting memorial to the Ritchie family's keen interest in the heritage of the island.

A more ambitious plan to found an 'Iona Celtic College', an idea which was to rumble on in various guises over the next decade, first made headlines in 1924. That year Angus Robertson, president of An Comunn Gaidhealach, went to New York to meet with the American Iona Society. This had been formed by businessmen with a nostalgic, but no doubt genuinely felt, concern for the Highland culture which their emigrant antecedents had left behind. Several observers of the time praised the intentions of those behind the scheme but, like Professor W. J. Watson addressing the Gaelic Society of Inverness in 1927, they felt that efforts might be better directed towards sustaining existing education and industry in the Highlands. Another speaker that evening picked up on the same theme but added a territorial claim, namely that if such a college were ever established it could only have one site – the banks of the Ness! In fact, Iona was merely lending its name and historical associations to the notion. There was an initial expectation, but no more than a fleeting one, that it might be located on the island itself. In any case, by the end of the 1920s the economic depression in America forced a halt – for the time being – to the Society's fund-raising plans.

The earlier notion that the cathedral might serve as a kind of theological college took further shape as a result of the divinity student retreats which began in 1920. The patron of these annual events, although this was not public knowledge for many years, was Dr David Russell of the Tullis Russell paper mills at Markinch in Fife. This philanthropic and far-sighted businessman, of wide interests, had first visited Iona in 1881 and was to buy Cnoc Mòr house in 1932 as a holiday base.

For a week each April, up to thirty third-year men from the four divinity halls in Scotland came to Iona for a programme of study,

Figure 12   Divinity students on retreat, 1926, snapped by Alex G. Fortune.
Seated in the middle are Professors W. P. Paterson, W. G. MacGregor and
G. S. Duncan. Photograph by courtesy of the Russell Trust and St Andrews
University Library.

discussion and worship. They were under the guidance of leading
theologians of the day, including Professor W. P. Paterson of New
College in Edinburgh, Professor Archibald Main of Glasgow and
Professor W. M. MacGregor of the United Free Church College in
Glasgow. All were enthusiastic about this chance to strengthen the
sense of fellowship amid the ranks of future ministers from across
the country and to build links between the sister churches.

On a personal level too it was highly beneficial. All students wrote a
letter to Dr Russell upon their return and these simple but sincere
expressions of gratitude are an often moving testimony to the enormous success of the whole experiment. 'Believe me, Sir, you have given
me a pearl of great price for which you have my constant indebtedness'
wrote one. Many stressed how appropriate they had found the peaceful atmosphere of the island and what a deep impression had been left

by the communion service in the ancient cathedral. Nor were they oblivious to their surroundings: 'Iona is beautiful for its own self ... the most wonderful thing about it is the song of the skylark, I think there must be hundreds of them. And all the isle is starred with old white farms.'

The students' afternoons were free, for walking, exploring and playing golf, which became an annual challenge to beat an islanders' team. And each year they put on a concert of music, recitations and humorous sketches which was always hugely popular with the local people. It was described to Dr Russell in 1928: 'To the villagers this was undoubtedly the chief event in our retreat and I was told by one of them that the children would be singing the songs they heard at it for the next year. Hamish MacKenzie got up the programme which lasted two and three-quarter hours ...!' They took a collection which went to a local cause, for example to the War Memorial Fund the first year. It was customary for the visiting ministers to take part in the Sunday worship, at the Church of Scotland service in the morning and in the United Free Church (formerly the Free Church) at Martyrs Bay in the evening. Both congregations turned out in large numbers, alongside the students, to hear these distinguished preachers.

For the first few years the party hired a steamer from Oban, the *Princess Louise*, for the last leg of the journey. But after a stormy passage in 1927 when many were seasick, they took the shorter scheduled crossing to Craignure and hired seven Ford motor cars in which they chugged across Mull. Accommodation was at first in the Argyll Hotel and from 1923 in the St Columba Hotel, where each retreat entry in the visitors' book vies with the preceding one for lavish embellishment. The occasional burst of verse also captures the good-natured enjoyment of the week:

> Columba in his devout career
> Fared hard and slept on flagstones chilly.
> For us glad lodging and good cheer
> Beneath the sign of Columcille!

The names entered in the twenty years the retreat ran consecutively include several who were to become well known in the ministry and would maintain a close personal assocation with Iona, for example

Leonard Small, Uist MacDonald, Hugh O. Douglas, Hamish Mac-
Intyre. During all this time, the travel and hotel expenses were met by
Dr Russell. The idea that the dormitory and refectory might one day
serve as lodging for the students was an obvious one, 'often mooted'
according to the Revd George Hendrie, minister of Dalmellington,
who wrote to Professor Paterson about it in 1926. His suggestion was
that the buildings be used the rest of the season by ministers of all the
Churches, who often found accommodation hard to book in a place so
popular with visitors. He knew of a minister from a Non-Conformist
Church in Manchester who was eager to begin collecting money for
the scheme without delay.

For the moment, however, Professor Paterson had a structure of less
tangible form in view. That year he and his colleagues decided to found
the Iona Fellowship, open to any who took part in the retreats. They
would resolve to set aside time for prayer and recollection of their Iona
experience each April and they would arrange reunions at suitable
intervals. By 1930, they had printed a short set of rules and appointed
a small advisory committee, of which Dr Russell was the Honorary
Secretary. It was not intended to be a movement that in itself would
create great waves; rather the emphasis was on fellowship and on continuing individual service to the Church. But the origins were considered significant and for the new group to have 'a national character and
an historic setting the association with Iona is of vital importance'.

On 2 October 1929, a formal ceremony in Edinburgh marked the
reunion of the Church of Scotland and the United Free Church of
Scotland. On Iona, in July of that year, the two denominations had
already held a joint service of thanksgiving for the recovery from illness
of King George V. It was described as the largest gathering ever seen
in the cathedral and the preacher, from Claremont United Free
Church in Glasgow, referred to Iona's hallowed associations with the
earliest kings of Scotland.

At first the united congregation used the church at Martyrs Bay, as
the Telford building, little used since the restoration of the cathedral
church, was in need of extensive repair – as also was the manse. The
vacancy caused by Mr MacMillan's illness from 1928, and his eventual
retirement in 1930, gave the Highlands and Islands Committee of the
Church an opportunity to consider both the problem of the parish

properties and that of securing a higher stipend. The endowment of £120 a century before, under the parliamentary grant, had not kept pace with the times. A public appeal was launched in 1932 under the auspices of a committee headed by the Moderator and which included several Iona Cathedral Trustees and other eminent ministers. Alex Ritchie was in charge of local collections and Honorary Treasurer was Sir John M. MacLeod, father of the Revd George F. MacLeod who was also a member. Dr David Russell took a close interest in the preparation of the appeal booklet, contributing to it a historical table in order to reinforce the importance of Iona in the story of the Scottish church. Two thousand booklets were printed, for sale on bookstalls and on board the Oban passenger steamers. In 1933, the Revd Donald MacCuish was appointed first minister of the united charge and by 1939 renovations to the parish church were completed. The interior remains attractive, in its simplicity, but it is perhaps regrettable that several hallmarks of the Telford design were removed at this stage – the pulpit with its precentor's desk, between the two windows of the south wall, and the long communion table in the centre of the boxed pews.

In 1935, the former United Free Church was put on the market and bought by Dr Isabel F. Grant, to house her embryonic collection of Highland artefacts. It was a useful location for her purposes since what she found on her forays among the inner and outer isles could be shipped by the *Dunara* direct to Iona for storage. A few things came from Iona itself, for example an iron swee, from which were hung cooking vessels over an open fireplace; a white cotton mutch, worn by women; a wooden toddy ladle; a cow hobble used when milking in the open air and woven from horse-hair by John MacMillan. By 1939, however, the museum had outgrown the small building and Dr Grant moved it to the mainland, first to Laggan and then to its permanent home in Kingussie.

Dr Grant's Gaelic name for her Highland Folk Museum was 'Am Fasgadh', the shelter. She had become convinced of the need to provide a refuge for objects and implements of all kinds which were being overtaken by modernisation and changing customs and which might otherwise just be thrown away. Simple tools, articles of clothing, pieces of kitchen ware and a myriad other items might demonstrate to future generations – in a more vital way than mere words could – something of how Highlanders had actually lived and worked. Although she did not know it, the decade when Dr Grant set to her task was a prelude to the country's second great watershed this century. Again, people would look back to these pre-war years as a time after which things would never be quite the same.

Seen from the outside, rural areas and the Highlands and Islands in particular tended to be pictured firmly in a past era. Literature of this period abounds in romantic rambles through these quaint and peaceful backwaters, from the pens of Halliday Sutherland, Alistair Alpin MacGregor, T. Ratcliffe Barnett and a dozen others. On the inside, the reality was more complex. Notwithstanding the degree of material improvement they had begun to enjoy, crofting areas were hit by the trickle-down effect of the worldwide trade slump as livestock prices fell, the fishing industry slumped and unemployment rose among merchant seamen. Thousands emigrated from Lewis; St Kilda was evacuated; and rapid depopulation threatened the social fabric of many small communities.

As earlier passages have indicated, however, Iona was relatively well protected from the worst of these problems during the 1920s and 1930s. Its good land and reasonably sized holdings provided a basic foothold and visitor-related income held steady. In common with much of the Highlands, the island's population showed a sharp dip in 1931, down to 141, although it should be noted that the 1921 figure of 234 may have been slightly inflated by visitors, since that census was taken in June instead of in the usual month of April.

The snapshots in these chapters of life on Iona during the inter-war decades may seem to reflect an unrealistically rosy glow. But talking over the last ten years to people familiar with the island then is, of necessity, to draw on a child's eye view. It is natural, perhaps, to remember the good and enjoyable days of childhood more readily than the dull or sorrowful ones, but this sifting process does not invalidate such memories. Iona was clearly a community which conveyed a strong sense of security and happiness to those growing up within it, and showed openness and kindness to those who came to know it. The frequency with which long-term visitors confirm these impressions is striking. And the degree to which their commitment to the island brought benefits of several different kinds is equally manifest.

As in earlier generations, a youngster's day consisted of work as well as play. Angie MacKay was a teenager when he went to help at Clachanach and a conversation recorded with him in late 1984, a few months before he died, swung readily between accounts of the two.

> I had to take the two horses out every day, for a drink to the burn – I used to jump on one's back and the other would come behind me. The year the two horses had a foal each was a nuisance, because if you were mowing or anything you had to put the wee foal in, in case he would get his feet cut with the mower; he got very wise for it. ... In the morning you had to go and see the beasts in the East End hills and feed them there or over in Calva ... and then there was the road to do, anywhere it needed doing. Sometimes you went down for wrack and if there was no wrack you just got gravel for the road. You had plenty to do.

Then there were pranks at Hallowe'en, being chased by Sandy Ruadh over the Machair after pinching his cart. Or on frosty moonlight nights the boys might go over to Calva, to slide about in their tackety boots where the waterlogged turf had turned to ice.

Elizabeth Kirkpatrick, brought up at Ruanaich, would remind her family if they had been for a walk to Port a' Churaich that she had had to go out to those hills before school, to milk the cows. Mary MacMillan from Lagnagiogan also tramped the West End pasture many a time to fetch in the cows, or was set to churning butter after coming home from school, a task she did not like. But she recalled that the girls too had fun at Hallowe'en:

> Well I remember that we always used to go out dressed up, the girls as well as the boys. It was on 11 November all through my youth – we went round a good many of the houses. One night Flora MacPhail and I dressed up and we removed Duncan MacGillivray's gate, just down to the Ruanaich fence and wasn't he furious the next day! He didn't know it was us ...

Schooling continued to be good and to develop its own local eccentricities. Pupils who went on to Oban High School in 1923 found themselves well ahead already in subjects such as arithmetic and science.

Figure 13 Catriona MacArthur feeding a lamb at Clachanach, 1934. She went to Glasgow to train as a children's nurse, but died in 1936, aged 20, after a short illness.

Ewen MacCormick, who had Iona connections and was schoolmaster from 1921 to 1925, had an imaginative and practical approach. He set geometry exercises using outdoor landmarks, taking pupils round the golf course with a measuring chain for example and getting them to calculate the height and angles of the nunnery walls. He gave them crosswords to extend their vocabulary, set up mock parliamentary elections and asked the pupils to organise their own referendum to decide whether they wanted to keep Hallowe'en at the old-style date or join the rest of the world in celebrating it on 31 October. The school garden lay just north of the nunnery and Angus MacPhail's prize effort of a tulip with five blooms on one stem made national news in June 1922, courtesy of a photograph in *The Bulletin*.

For children brought up in the village, such as May MacLeod, the summer in particular was a time when they virtually lived in the open air. There were chores at home too of course. When her baby brother was teething, May's mother often sent her to the shore for a piece of tangle, a bit from the young pliable stem for him to chew on. He was given a fresh one every day. The shoreline was primarily, however, a playground.

The girls would 'do the rocks', an exercise in good balance as they leaped nimbly from one to the next right along below the street until they reached the Bishop's House. Beyond there lay the Liana Mhòr, open grassland strewn with boulders to climb and with flat rocks ideal for acting out 'wee houses'. Many a sandpie decorated with seaweed was 'cooked' there and dock seeds gathered to make 'lentil' soup. Many of their games were those played by children everywhere – tig, hide and seek, kick the can and ball-beds, their version of the universal hopscotch. Years later, May could still describe this in detail:

> You make a square of nine and you mark them, number them. You need a nice flat piece of ground for it. And you roll your ball into one and you go into it and you bounce one; then you go back and roll your ball into two and bounce two and so on, right round the nine. There was some rule about not letting the ball go out of the square or the next person gets a turn. And when you've done the nine, if you still haven't been put out you can choose a bed and

Figure 14 Children, including one or two MacPhails, playing on the shore
*c.*1910. The Carraig Fhada, the long rock that used to serve as a rough jetty,
is in the background. Photograph taken by Elsie M. Ogilvie, courtesy of
Antonia Maclean.

put a cross in it and no-body can go in it … so you have to leap.
Oh it goes on and on, day after day … it was a good game!

There were also distractions peculiar to Iona that helped mark out
the passing seasons vividly for the children. The divinity students' concert at Easter, mentioned earlier, was one. The day the coal puffer
came in early summer was another, and then there was the arrival of
the tinkers, often about the beginning of June. These were usually
MacAllisters who sailed round from Tobermory in their own skiff. The
parents and children set up camp, sometimes below Clachanach where
they could dig a few potatoes for their own use, and other times at
Martyrs Bay where their tents were soon crowded with small extras, in
the shape of local youngsters pleased to meet up with their pals again.
The MacAllisters were well known and respected in the area, mending
pails and milk-cans before travelling on.

Sunday was not a day for recreation. But if the afternoon was good, a passer-by might have seen, and heard, up to fifty children lined up inside the walls of the nunnery ruins. This was the summer Sunday School which visiting ministers, including Robert Ritchie when he came home on holiday, helped to organise. The small harmonium was brought out from the school, to make a joyful noise.

When the pleasure steamers ceased running in early September, there was a distinct change of pace on the island. Virtually no visitors came out of season. And in the MacLeod household another sign of approaching winter was when a parcel of lace-up boots for May, and tackety boots for her brothers, arrived at their mother's shop.

Seton Gordon the naturalist, another prolific observer of Hebridean life in the inter-war years but one who wrote about it more realistically than some, knew Mull and Iona well. In *Highways and Byways in the West Highlands*, published in 1935, he pondered a few signs of change: 'Iona, remote as it is, begins to feel the influence of this modern age. The Gaelic language is dying out. No longer does the old ferryman, Coll Maclean, sail out from Fionphort in his well-tried skiff … motor boats without the charm of sail, have taken his place.'

Moving to motor boats for their daily link with Mull was the kind of progress which the islanders themselves had argued for and welcomed. That the engine was less picturesque than unfurled canvas concerned them little.

The decline in Gaelic, and in the songs and stories that went with it, will have been a change much more keenly felt, by some at least. Others may well have been influenced by the prevailing ethos through-out the country, only very recently countered with any success, that the language had no useful place anyway in 'this modern age'. The turning-point may be seen graphically within the Clachanach family. The elder three children spoke only Gaelic until they went to school, but by the time the younger three were of school age, in the mid-1920s, they could already speak English.

Meanwhile, practical advances inched the island forward into line with the mainland. The last of the thatched cottages were roofed with slates or built up. The first house to incorporate a bathroom had prob-ably been Greenbank, when it was renovated and raised to two storeys back around 1910. Others gradually followed suit and in the mid-1930s several took advantage of grants under the Housing (Rural Workers) Act to instal hot and cold water, sinks and a bath. There was as yet no public reservoir, however. Householders built their own tanks from which to pump a supply, while extra came from rainwater butts and drinking water was still usually brought from the nearest well.

The first wireless set was brought to Traighmòr in 1923, a curious contraption which sat outside while the Cameron girls were photographed listening to it through headphones. Angus MacPhail, postmaster for thirty-five years, County Councillor and Justice of the Peace, died in 1931 shortly before the first telephone was connected to the Post Office. It remained the only one for most of the decade. At the General Election of 1924 the islanders had their own polling booth for the first time, instead of having to go to Bunessan to vote, largely thanks to the campaigning efforts of Sergeant Donald Black.

The paddle-steamer era on the Oban–Staffa–Iona route finally ended in 1931, when the *Fusilier* bowed out to make way for the newly launched *Lochfyne*. She in turn moved on in 1936 and was replaced by the *King George V*, to become well loved by future generations of passengers. Day tourists were in effect those who landed from the Oban steamer for a couple of hours and then sailed away again. A portent of future mass-movement of tourists over much longer distances came that same year when British Rail advertised their longest day excursion ever planned. For 35/- you could travel over 1,000 miles from London to Staffa and Iona, and back again thirty-six hours later.

The wonders of aviation were introduced briefly to Iona when a private plane landed on the Machair above Port Bàn. School emptied in a trice at the electrifying sounds overhead. Iain MacCormick remembers a swarm of delighted boys tracking it from Calva where the pilot first circled: 'We were so fast on those hills that we managed to reach it just as the engine stopped.' Later, around 1933, two seaplanes – *Cloud of Iona* and *Cloud of Soa* – brought passengers on a flight from Oban and landed them at Martyrs Bay.

In the early 1920s, an article in the *Oban Times* extolling the charms of Iona suggested that St Columba was not necessarily the chief attraction. The writer was certain that his fellow-visitors were drawn to the island partly by its natural beauty and partly by 'the present and interesting company of still living people' whom they were bound to meet there. He was evidently a stalwart of some seasons' standing as he mentioned the diversion of stepping into the Post Office, either 'for a crack with Angus' or to blether with others while waiting for the mail, this event being 'one of the island's modern entertainments'.

It was undoubtedly true that Iona was by now much more than a historic site for large numbers of people. Yet its place at the heart of the Christian church in Scotland held true in at least equal measure. And worship remained central, too, to the local congregation. The first radio broadcast from Iona Cathedral was a Gaelic service on Sunday 7 June 1936, conducted by the Revd Donald MacCuish and supported by the Tobermory Gaelic Choir. A Mrs Johnston, who with her husband was a regular visitor, had the idea of scattering fish in the grounds to attract seagulls. This simple method of creating appropriate island sound effects was to be copied for many future broadcasts.

In his sermon, the parish minister spoke of the light of faith which had come to Iona with Colum Cille and had gone forth from it again, winning high regard and divine blessing for this small place down the centuries. The generation to come, Mr MacCuish continued, might see even better things. Who knew what yet could happen here for, in the words attributed to the saint:

> An I mo chridhe, I mo ghràidh
> An àite guth manaich bidh geum bà
> Ach mun tig an saoghal gu crìch
> Bidh I mar a bha.

Iona shall be as it was. Before long there was to be another reason for people to come to the island. Soon, the famous saying was to be adopted in a fresh context by an unknown undertaking, and this new strand in Iona's story was to bring significant and permanent change.

14

A New Community in Iona

'There's to be a new community in Iona'. Dugald MacArthur was working in Glasgow when he heard this from his close friend Johnnie MacInnes, who had read it in the newspaper. It was late April 1938. The Revd George F. MacLeod, minister of Govan Old Parish Church, had announced his plans for a novel experiment in Christian witness and worship, an integral part of which would be the rebuilding of the monastic ruins adjacent to Iona Cathedral. The new grouping to undertake the task would be known as 'The Iona Community'. Although this news was sprung without warning on the island, on the national media and on the Church of Scotland at large – to the irritation of some at the General Assembly which met the next month – action had been happening behind the scenes for some time. And the cast of players was a complicated one.

That most, or even all, of the island's ecclesiastical remains might one day be fully restored was tentatively advanced at an early stage by the Iona Cathedral Trust. Its very first appeal leaflet, in 1904, pointed to the aim of eventually repairing the chapter-house, the cloisters and St Oran's Chapel as well as the church itself. Ideas for the use of the residential part of the complex had already been brought to its attention. All of the trustees, however, had full-time responsibilities in their own spheres and there was little sign, as the 1920s had worn on, that they would be able to push forward very rapidly any new initiatives for the Iona sites. It was understandable that impetus was more likely to come from outside the Trust.

One who had maintained a keen interest from the outset was Dr David Russell, patron of the divinity student retreats. Early in 1931 he asked the trustees if he might submit to them suggestions for further restoration and expressed his willingness to assist with fund-raising, should such plans go ahead. Two months later, almost certainly prompted by Russell's ideas, the trustees applied for support to a public trust, opening with the statement: 'There are adjoining the Cathedral a number of most interesting monastic buildings, presently in a state of ruin, which we have all long hoped would some day be put into a proper state of repair.' They added their hope that a rest-house for the use of city ministers might be incorporated.

The application was not successful and in Russell's view it had been put together a little too hastily. Meanwhile, and at his own cost, he had engaged architect Reginald Fairlie to draw up a design for the Iona monastic buildings. Fairlie had been in charge of the restoration of St Salvator's Chapel in St Andrews. All this was happening in tandem with the appeal, set in train in 1931 and in which David Russell was also prominent, to raise funds both for the Parish Church and the incoming minister's stipend. And privy to these various efforts was the new minister in Govan.

The initial phase of the cathedral restoration was only just underway when George MacLeod first visited Iona as a boy of 9, in 1904. The family holidayed there regularly, and in the late 1930s George acted as a leader on the Easter divinity student retreats. In a letter to him in November 1931, Russell doubted the wisdom of trying to put out the double parish appeal *plus* a cathedral buildings appeal. This was despite an optimistic note sounded by George a few months before: 'I have not any doubt that even in these times we could get almost anything we want for Iona provided we backed the right scheme.' In the event, the parish appeal went ahead in 1932 but it was not until December 1933 that the trustees officially considered the Fairlie drawings. Present at that meeting was official guide Alex Ritchie, whose brother Robert had left the bequest for the Celtic library within the cathedral. It was agreed that part of this could go towards a caretaker's or librarian's house. But no concrete progress appears to have been made.

In the autumn of 1935 things began to stir again. The American Iona

Society reappeared on the scene, having announced to the press early in 1931 plans to relaunch their appeal for a college in the Scottish Highlands with a target of two million pounds. Again this seemed but a straw in the wind until, in October 1935, they made a formal approach to the Iona Cathedral Trust for permission to rebuild the remaining ruins as a worship and study retreat. The Revd Charles Warr, minister of St Giles and chairman of the trustees, sent them a copy of the Fairlie drawings and expressed the hope to David Russell that their idea 'might be worked in with the Revd George MacLeod's scheme for a community settlement'. The latter was invited to a trustees' meeting the following month when agreement in principle was given to the Americans' proposal. Important conditions were attached, however, namely that the trustees would have to retain sole management over the buildings and would first have to receive sufficient funds.

Also circulated that day was a memorandum outlining a quite separate proposal. In his work in city parishes, amid the misery of the depression years, George MacLeod had become convinced that the Church had drifted too far from the harsh realities of life for many ordinary folk, particularly in the sprawling new urban fringes. He had conceived the idea of a brotherhood, as it was first called, in which young ministers would engage in some task of physical renewal alongside skilled workmen before carrying the message of spiritual renewal back to their parishes. These themes would combine ideally on Iona: 'The craftsmen to restore the Cathedral while the first group prepared themselves for their work ... a Cathedral so restored would itself be a sermon of the modern vitality of our church life ... and worth ten Cathedrals restored by normal business contract.'

The notion of an Iona College received quite wide publicity and generated not a little controversy. Angus Robertson, who had been closely in touch with the American Iona Society a decade before, again gave them his active support. A *Sunday Express* headline waxed lyrical: 'World Centre of Celtic Art and Culture. A Man's 10-year Dream.' Although the cultural legacy of Iona continued to be presented as the basic inspiration behind the scheme, it was soon accepted that for practical reasons the actual site ought to be on the mainland. There was a flurry of claims as to eminent suitability from divers localities the length and breadth of the Highlands. That such a campus should, however, be linked to some kind of spiritual centre or retreat house on Iona itself remained part of the deal, and when George MacLeod and Angus Robertson met, late in 1935, they agreed that their two schemes could be entirely complementary.

Towards the end of 1936, yet another player entered the arena. Mr Clare Vyner, the owner of Fountains Abbey in North Yorkshire, had seen Reginald Fairlie's designs for Iona at the Royal Society of Arts. His family had owned Torloisk House for a period, and acquaintance-ship with Mull had left him disheartened about the future for much of the West Highlands. Community life was declining, much practical knowledge was in danger of dying out and the Church, on its own, did not seem able to tackle the decay. He wrote at length to David Russell, suggesting that the Iona buildings be used to bring together theological study *and* training for young men in fields such as agriculture, fishing, gardening and weaving. After two years, during which the trainees might also visit other countries for useful experience, they would go out into parishes or lay occupations equipped to bring 'a real militant Christianity to bear on the problems that are always being presented'.

There is no record that Vyner had any knowledge of George MacLeod's ideas, yet aspects of each scheme chime together with uncanny closeness. George's initial reaction, however, was mildly dis-paraging. He wrote in confidence to Russell that he was not impressed by 'a vaguely Christian social scheme' of a type which he considered had had its day: 'Stormier clouds are on the horizon and what alone will stand up to the next two decades is *The* Faith.'

Clare Vyner continued to develop his ideas nevertheless, in further correspondence with David Russell and at a meeting with several of the Iona Cathedral Trustees in January 1937. There was brief specula-tion about using Burg Farm on the far side of Loch Scridain in Mull as the site for practical training but this was rejected on grounds of distance. It was beginning to look as if there might be two schemes, closely linked, a prospect which George MacLeod was now willing to embrace more enthusiastically. He thought that a centre of agriculture and crafts would be 'an essential ancillary' to his more spiritually oriented project and might prevent it becoming 'an ecclesiastical back-water'. In February 1937, Vyner finally managed to get to Govan. After a talk with George he reported to David Russell: 'The major issue of Iona seems to be very much in MacLeod's hands ... If he goes ahead with his idea it will be a very alive business – obviously a concrete scheme and as such is probably the one to hope for.' This implies a tacit withdrawal by Vyner and no record has been found of any further action on his part.

Meanwhile, the cathedral trustees had been attempting to pin down their transatlantic contacts as to how concrete was their progress in raising funds. A letter dated 5 May 1937 indicated with regret that the Trust might expect nothing financially from the American Iona Society and that the matter should be considered closed.

There was now, in effect, only one proposal on the table. George MacLeod energetically pursued possible sponsors and refined the details of the paper finally laid before the trustees on 7 March 1938. They gave their approval, the sponsors held their first meeting, in strict confidence, exactly one month later and a press release was issued on 26 April.

The setting up of the Iona Community represented a huge leap of faith for its founder. He left the relative security of the Govan charge, where his reputation for charismatic preaching and humane ministry had strengthened, and embarked upon an untested venture for which, moreover, he had to find all the money. The cathedral trustees had made it clear that no financial responsibility was to devolve on to them. And although the sponsors included several well-known and respected clergymen, some of the severest criticism of the new body, almost from the very start, came from within the Church of Scotland.

The full story of the fund-raising, the rebuilding, the obstacles along the way and the people involved has been told by the Revd Ronald Ferguson in *Chasing the Wild Goose*, a history of the Iona Community, and in *George MacLeod*, the authorised biography. The focus of the latter book, naturally, is the man himself, the events and traits of character that shaped him, the principles that motivated him. The task of this book is to relay, as far as is possible, the impact of this new organisation and powerful personality on the life of the island itself.

A place already so famous in its own right, and with a large adopted population scattered throughout the land in addition to its residential one, was clearly going to come under a spotlight at the first hint of discord. 'Iona's Peace is Shattered! First Motor Lorry on Island' screamed an *Evening Times* headline in August 1938. The subheading, also in large print, was 'Residents' and Visitors' Resentment'.

The age of motor vehicles was going to dawn sooner or later, even on the Sacred Isle, but the fact that it was ushered in by the Iona Community was bound to draw fire. Reaction was not without its humorous side. At one of the regular fancy-dress dances in the hall, a participant wore half a navy-blue pullover and one trouser leg, representing the uniform of the newcomers, while his other arm and leg were in blazer and shorts. He pulled a toy car on a string and called himself 'Iona Divided'. And it was a local horse and cart that came to the rescue when the lorry got stuck in the sands for the first time.

The divisions were not, of course, clear-cut. A letter to *The Bulletin* that first summer from eight young people, all regular visitors, defended what they termed a 'sign of life and adventure in our church' and claimed that the Iona experiment would deepen and not destroy the charm of the isle. An anonymous newspaper article asked if there might not be a separate scheme for women and had heard a rumour that the ruined nunnery might be the very place, although local information was that such an idea would spoil a perfectly lovely garden.

One of the earliest setbacks was the Duke of Argyll's refusal to allow the Community access to a water supply outside the cathedral precincts, on the ground which he still owned. Now passed into their internal mythology, and granted near-miracle status, is the story of the water diviners summonsed to search for a source inside the walls while an advance party erected the accommodation huts for the first recruits, due to arrive in July 1938. Nothing was found but on the day of their departure the steamer was late and it was in that extra hour or so that they stumbled upon a plentiful spring of water in the depths of what they called a 'round tower' in front of the cathedral's west door.

Locals were at best baffled and at worst derisive, for everyone knew that this was a well, a good well which never ran dry. Indeed, it was quite common for the MacKenzies at the nearby Columba Hotel to draw on it in a prolonged dry spell when their own supply was not sufficient. This was not a major episode in itself. But it was a first small sign of the kind of gap, whether in information or attitude, that was to open up more painfully between the two communities in the years ahead.

The second summer brought several incidents which caused immediate outcry. The upper part of the manse glebe had been loaned to the Community as a vegetable garden and an over-zealous employee took it upon himself to breach the old wall near Maclean's Cross to gain easier access to the ground. He also attempted to burn out the rookery in the manse trees, as the birds stood accused of plundering the vegetables. Both the parish minister and George MacLeod were attending the General Assembly at the time and on their return the wall was swiftly repaired. There were outraged letters to the press about the 'Slaughter of the Rooks', damage which was less easy to put right.

By a curious coincidence, the Scottish Society for the Protection of Wild Birds had recently lobbied the County Council to have Iona declared a bird sanctuary but without success. The Council had felt that such designation was not suited to a crofting island which needed to keep the right to kill birds, if necessary, to protect crops. The Society's Secretary seized on the news of the rooks' fate to justify further the need for a bird Protection Order on Iona. His initial argument that the measure was appropriate had leaned heavily, and slightly improbably, on the 'refined and religious atmosphere' of the place where Columba had once cared for a wounded crane, thus creating a sanctuary for birds as well as pilgrims. Nothing came of the Protection Order and in course of time the rookery recovered.

An even more prolonged correspondence was occasioned by the decision, sanctioned by the Cathedral Trust and the Office of Works, to use stones from the boundary walls in the rebuilding. In the event, this did not happen. Amid all the indignation one letter, signed 'Staffa', offered an acute understanding of what the fuss was really about. In a way it was logical enough that stone long ago taken out of the original structure might be replaced in its modern reincarnation. But long association can confer a sense of permanence and the natives of Iona had simply come to regard the wall as an integral part of the old precincts, thus not something to tamper with lightly. Anyone trying to introduce modernisation into these parts, warned 'Staffa', would do well to pay due regard to Highland sentiment: 'It need not be a barrier, but rather a guide-post to the correct course to follow.' It was perceptive advice.

At the individual and personal level, naturally enough, the additional summer influx of craftsmen and young ministers got on well with many islanders and regular visitors. They joined in football matches, dances and concerts; friendships were formed, several marriages made. During the first two seasons, Community members visited all the island households to talk about what they were doing.

None the less, the perceived disruptions or interferences were genuinely felt and although some may have been little more than minor irritations, the accumulative effect was considerable. Yet another small incident during 1939 pointed towards what was going to cause the most profound, if least publicised, hurt among the local community. A letter to the press complained about the men's washing flapping in the breeze on a Sunday. Then a lady wrote directly to the Community in support and enclosed a large donation, remarking that cleanliness was next to godliness. And so they always hung their washing out on a Sunday after that. Again, this story has passed into the Iona Community's own annals as one of George MacLeod's favourite anecdotes, guaranteed to raise a smile.

In the late 1930s, and indeed for many years after that, Sundays were strictly observed on Iona as days of rest and worship. No one hung out their washing. In retrospect it seems an extraordinary lapse in simple courtesy, if not in the tactics of establishing neighbourly relations, to have risked such certain offence. And to make of it a long-standing joke merely reinforces the lack of sensitivity. It was a rift over Sunday worship itself, however, that was to prove almost intractable over the next several years.

The minute of the first meeting of the Iona Community sponsors had noted that the parish minister of Iona would be an *ex officio* sponsor, although the Revd Donald MacCuish's name was not among the list of those present on that occasion. Neither he nor the Kirk Session had any inkling of the new scheme until it was announced. As had been their custom since 1905, the congregation used the cathedral during the summer months for two services each Sunday, at noon and at half past six. The Community began to hold two services each day, early morning and late evening and a Sunday morning one at ten o'clock, to

all of which local people and the usual large number of visitors were
warmly invited. Some did attend, out of real interest or politeness or
curiosity; others did not. There were also joint occasions now and
again, such as broadcasts or services near to 9 June in commemoration
of St Columba's Day.

Although strictly speaking the cathedral was not their parish church,
customary usage had led to a certain proprietary sense towards it
on the part of the islanders. Therefore, changes in which they were
not consulted, such as the introduction by the Community of new
furnishings, plus the shifting of others, must have been unsettling if
not actively resented. As for the services themselves, exploring new
ways of worship was central to what George MacLeod was trying to do.
He believed that the Protestant church had lost sight of strands in its
own pre-Reformation heritage that many were now seeking to reinterpret. Inevitably, some of this was bound to seem strange, even
downright heretical, to a strongly traditional Presbyterian congregation. In April 1940, the parish minister and Session Clerk wrote to the
cathedral trustees criticising the Iona Community's form of service.
While Mr MacCuish was reassured that his permission to use the
church in summer was not affected, the trustees hoped that he and Dr
MacLeod might come to some compromise over joint Sunday worship
or continue their separate services.

In the event, Donald MacCuish was shortly to move on from the
charge. He was a mild-mannered man and not openly antagonistic
towards the dynamic clergyman who had burst upon his parish.
Indeed, he confided to an islander that he had felt sorry for George
MacLeod at that year's General Assembly, when the former soldier's
pacifist views were virtually shouted down. Mr MacCuish was, however, deeply troubled by the pattern of events unfolding from the
hutted settlement in the shade of the cathedral walls. At the final meeting with his elders he advised them to remain firm and look out for
their own interests. One of them nodded in agreement and recalled
that it was they who had first warned him.

The charge was vacant over the next eighteen months but neither
side was idle. George MacLeod wrote at length in October 1940 to the
Revd Charles Warr, chairman of the trustees, urging him to clarify
the situation before the next minister was appointed. He pointed out

that he himself had never failed to attend parish services, some of which Iona Community ministers had been invited to conduct, but that such participation was not reciprocated by all. He thought that attendance and therefore collections at the parish services were lower, and surmised – correctly – that this was one source of annoyance. He felt that the 'uncertainty' of the elders did not reflect general attitudes. The ideal solution, in his view, was for the Trust to delegate management of services in the cathedral to the Iona Community, who would then 'strain every nerve' to induce the parish minister and congregation to join it in worship.

In the same month, the Kirk Session also wrote to the trustees, enclosing a copy of a minute it had sent to the Presbytery of Mull. This stated that it was 'profoundly perturbed' by developments on the island and posed the question: was it in accordance with the law of the Church of Scotland that Holy Communion be celebrated, and collections taken up, in any parish without the knowledge or consent of the minister of that parish?

It was a legitimate question and Charles Warr had to admit that in raising it the Kirk Session was on firm ground. Indeed, shortly afterwards, he regretfully withdrew as a sponsor of the Iona Community so as to avoid a possible clash of interests. For the position of the Iona Cathedral Trust was in fact very unclear. The Deed of Trust had appeared to grant the trustees power to decide who conducted worship within the cathedral, and included giving permission to the local minister to do so. Did that therefore suspend the normal law of the Church so that the Iona Community came directly under the trustees' jurisdiction, rather than that of the Mull Presbytery as would otherwise be assumed?

The Revd Murdo MacRae came to the Iona charge in May 1942 and immediately took up this question, still not satisfactorily answered. Eventually, in 1943, the Cathedral Trust sought legal advice. The counsel's verdict was that the late Duke of Argyll had indeed intended that the ordinary rights of the parish minister of Iona should not apply to worship in the cathedral. This was, in effect, to alter or suspend the law of the Church *but* the power to make any such change ought to have lain with the Church of Scotland alone. That the General Assembly had given its approval to the Deed of Trust did not alter the fact that, if the clause about conduct of worship was ever tested, the Duke's unofficial action had left the trustees in a weak position.

The response from the Iona Community leader was brisk. He would continue to assume that he did not require to ask permission of the parish minister to conduct worship; that they both had access to the cathedral at the discretion of the trustees; and that he would try, as before, to come to an amicable joint arrangement about Sunday services. Mr MacRae, however, was a more fiery and outspoken character than his predecessor. He shared the concerns of the elders – about the, to them, unorthodox style of worship, about Communion celebrated by someone from outside the Presbytery, about the sense of encroachment. An open-air service by the shore incensed him still further. Letters flew back and forth by the ream, to the Trust, to the Community, to every house on the island, to the newspapers.

And the minister grasped quite early two general consequences of the new venture which had already begun to cause local disquiet, and would long continue to do so. First, there was now confusion in the public mind over who had rebuilt what, leading to the assumption that the entire restoration – including the cathedral church – was because of George MacLeod's efforts. Secondly, there was a tendency to use 'Iona' as shorthand for 'the Iona Community', thus enforcing the impression that nothing else existed on the island. 'Let it be clearly stated and distinctly understood that the Iona Community is not "Iona"' wrote Mr MacRae in a letter to the *Oban Times* in 1944.

Not until the spring of 1945 was the matter of worship resolved. The trustees agreed to support the Kirk Session's proposals, the main element of which was that on the last Sunday of each month the cathedral be reserved for the parish Holy Communion and that no Iona Community service be held that day. Despite all George's offers of flexible co-operative arrangements, and these were not negligible, this conclusion was still a long step away from the dream he had several times expressed to Murdo MacRae – that new pilgrims to Iona would experience full worship every day, welcomed by neither of them as individual ministers 'but by the whole Household of the Faith on the island'.

During all of this undoubted aggravation for the fledgling organisation, unfailing encouragement came from David Russell. 'I am full of confidence but I feel that George MacLeod needs all the support we can give him,' he wrote early in 1939 to the Revd G. E. Troup. Another faithful visitor to Iona, Mr Troup had preached there often and knew the MacLeod family well. Although he admired George's abilities, he was saddened by the division in the parish and never became a member of the Iona Community himself.

Russell made generous donations towards the refurbishment programme and the development of the Community's wider work, and both moral and financial support were to continue in later years through his son – also David – and the family Trust. George incorporated the former Easter student retreats into his own programme and in one letter to Russell acknowledged that 'but for your quiet constancy in creating and maintaining these retreats, I doubt if I would be in Iona today or the scheme as far as it is'.

The regular, often daily, correspondence between them illustrates how steadfast was the friendship and how much it contributed to the growth of the project. MacLeod's biography makes clear how isolated he was, particularly during the dark days of the war when the Community was frequently, but unjustly, charged with shirking its duty. George held to the pacifist position he had come to but did not impose this on other Community members or staff. They had to make their own decision.

There were other bumps along the path. Before the second summer, and the first of full activity on the rebuilding, the architect Alastair MacQueen resigned. The Office of Works had rejected his wish to blend some modern elements into the reconstruction. Generously, MacQueen said that an older architect, with an established reputation, might be a 'safer' prospect for the Community. The Reginald Fairlie plans were resurrected and Ian Lindsay, who had done the original survey work on them, was appointed. Typically, George MacLeod fretted that this was a dull compromise, ending the exciting prospect of making a medieval building serve contemporary needs.

Another instance of an imaginative idea, but again one probably before its time, came in 1942 when George outlined to David Russell his vision of sending a boat to Oban every week, full of intensively grown vegetables for market, so bypassing freight charges. The

enterprise could be run co-operatively with crofters in the area, to
the benefit of all. This echo of the earlier Clare Vyner scheme arose
because George had submitted a bid for the tenancy of the St Columba
Hotel and farm, which the MacKenzies had just given up. Somewhat
to his indignation, the offer was not accepted.

Quite what the islanders would have made of such a venture had it
happened is intriguing to contemplate. 'They will end up taking over
everything' was a warning frequently repeated anyway. Yet it is not
impossible that linking up with some kind of work on the land might,
over time, have helped bridge the barriers. For barriers there undoubtedly were. The Iona Community leader did not read – or did not heed
– the advice offered by 'Staffa' during the boundary wall furore. The
body of beliefs and outlooks that go to make up 'Highland sentiment'
have been shaped over a long time and cannot be modified or replaced
overnight.

For someone who was no stranger to Iona, George MacLeod
seemed curiously out of touch in certain respects. Not until 1947,
after David Russell loaned him a copy of the newspaper cuttings, did
he learn of the 1892 controversy over the building of the Episcopal
chapel. This account of a much earlier disagreement between a parish
minister and the then owner of the cathedral afforded him a hearty
chuckle. But it is astonishing that he knew nothing of an affair that was
still well remembered locally and ought to have provided significant
pointers about religious attitudes within the parish. Nor can it have
occurred to him simply to enquire whether the arrival of an Episcopal
witness had caused any problems.

The people of Iona had long been accustomed to receiving visitors.
They had long been used to hearing different ministers in their pulpit,
especially since the rebuilding of the cathedral church. They warmly
welcomed back each year the group of young divinity students. And
they were by no means unfamiliar with disputes, whether with landlords or factors, councils or boards, or indeed among themselves. What
made the Iona Community so different was, first, that it *was* a community in itself. It was not merely a collection of individuals but a
group that was quickly to develop a corporate identity, a public voice,
a shared purpose. And its adoption of the place-name 'Iona' in its
own name may well have reinforced the islanders' sense that where

they lived was being somehow appropriated, that their very existence was being overshadowed.

Secondly, the personality of George MacLeod himself cannot be overlooked. In the biography, Ron Ferguson deals honestly with those facets of a complex character – his stubbornness and impatience, for example – which were less than easy to live and work with. Did the single-mindedness with which George felt he had to pursue his mission blind him to the real hurt caused along the way? Early in the worship dispute he wrote, revealingly: 'What bores me is the fear of these big men, whenever any issue arises that may cause trouble. As if there wasn't going to be a load of trouble anyway before the Church awakens to her opportunity …?' The impression is that although the local concerns could not be ignored, they were irksome; that there really was not time for them when the greater task lay ahead.

Yet 'these big men' were members of the same Church. The issues on which they proved so dogged centred on that expression of the Christian faith in which they had been brought up. Looking back from an age when ecumenism has become much more widely accepted, the attitudes of minister and Kirk Session then may today seem unduly conservative. But they were of their time and place. It was all very well for George MacLeod to claim 'that what happens in Iona is not an island affair but a national one'. For those who actually lived there, the emphasis was precisely the other way around.

Not that the islanders always made it easy for mutual understanding to blossom. David Russell felt that Archibald MacArthur, who was Kirk Session treasurer and had penned the first key statements of complaint, had long harboured a prejudice against George MacLeod. It may be that he did and the reasons may or may not have had reasonable foundation. But he was not alone in his concerns which were particularly, although not solely, about worship; they were deeply felt by many and left a lasting legacy. Archibald MacArthur himself died in 1941, several years before the question of the services was resolved.

Both Mr MacCuish and Mr MacRae, and all the elders of the time, were native Gaelic speakers. George MacLeod was not. His mother was English and on the other side a direct link with the language had been broken at his father's generation. Very few Gaels were ever closely involved in the Iona Community, particularly at the beginning, and it is impossible not to wonder if this might not have made a difference. For language is more than just a translated form of words; it reflects a particular cast of mind, another way of looking at the world. The minister justly famed for his 'common touch' in city streets and youth camps alike never did find an affinity, especially in those crucial early years, with most of the ordinary folk of Iona.

All of this makes the reading, today, of an article in *The Coracle* from the autumn of 1938 all the more strange – and more than a little poignant. This was the first issue of the magazine begun by the Community in response to a flood of requests for information about its purpose and activities. The piece was about local reaction to the new venture. It admitted that the islanders had been understandably cautious at the start of this experiment in their midst but, on realising that the Reformation was not going to be reversed after all, most had welcomed it and flocked to join in worship 'in their old Abbey which had become our common home'. Was this an exercise in wishful thinking based on an element of truth? – because it is certainly the case that a lot of visitors and some locals did attend services, initially at least. Or did a number show interest at the start but later changed their views? The writer ended on an optimistic note: 'From now on, in all we seek to do, we rest assured that the Iona Community seeks a common purpose and a common life with the Community of Iona.'

In no subsequent issue of the magazine was there a follow-up to this article, nor was there ever any reference to strained relations on the island. A common purpose and a common life never did transpire. Whether the two communities were the poorer for that, or whether it was all along an impossible vision, remains a moot point.

15

Protected Area Number Three

On an August evening in 1939 Dugald MacArthur took Alex and George Ritchie out to fish for lythe round Rèidhlean, off the west side of Iona. News on the international situation was gloomy. Alex remarked that this was the third time in his life the German people seemed set for war. As a teenager in 1870, after an all-night session fishing salmon with his father at Camas in Mull, he had come back into Iona jetty to hear that the Franco-Prussian War had broken out. During the First World War he was back from sea and living in Iona. Now it looked as if it was all going to start again.

Once more Mull and Iona became a protected area, Number Three, and permits to enter or leave it had to be shown at Oban pier. The summer passenger steamer *King George V* was dispatched to the Clyde to help transfer troops and she was also to take part in the evacuation at Dunkirk. Cargo services continued although the departure times could not be published and were often subject to delays. Iona was virtually cut off for eight days early in 1940 because of transport problems, mail and food left stranded at Craignure.

On the island a women's work party again set to knitting and the Woman's Guild organised Christmas gifts for local men serving in the forces. There were fund-raising events for the Red Cross, for the Spitfire Fund set up by the *Oban Times* and, in 1942, to adopt two prisoners of war on behalf of Mull and Iona. A depot was reopened in Oban to receive spaghnum moss.

Items in the *Oban Times* in September 1939 drew attention to the

Figure 15   Alex and George Ritchie fishing off Rèidhlean, 1939.
Photographed by Dugald MacArthur.

need for volunteers to assist with harvest, to the training underway for
a women's Land Army and to the fact that farmers would be subsidised
by two pounds per acre to plough up grassland for crops or potatoes.
Part of Calva's pasture was cultivated over the next few years, as was
the Columba field north of the cathedral. Two Land Army girls came
to the Columba farm towards the middle of the war; one also went to
Cùlbhuirg and another to Ruanaich. The school roll was boosted too as
a few evacuees came to island homes, mostly where they had a family
connection.

Rationing came in, of course, but as during the First World War
there continued to be a reasonable local supply of basic fresh foods. In
fact, surplus eggs sometimes found their way to worse-off homes in the
city, via the sailors on the cargo vessels who were glad to buy them. And
one or two such as Janet MacArthur, who used to order an entire
tea-box of Carrs' biscuits at a time, found that they still received a box
throughout the war – although a smaller one – as the firm was keen to
maintain the custom.

A Fuel Control Committee was set up under the County Council,
with Ian MacKenzie as the member from Iona, and later – in 1943 –
each household had to fill in forms from the Local Fuel Overseer

based in Dunoon, showing fuel usage for lighting, heating and cooking. Most people still relied heavily on kerosene and, of course, coal for their fires. Hector Maclean Sligineach acted as coal merchant at that time and kerosene was usually bought direct from MacFarlane Shearer in Greenock or through Martha MacLeod's shop. As before, the black-out was stringently applied.

Visitors continued to come despite the transport difficulties and the need to obtain permits. Day tourists were even catered for by Alex Cowe's 'cars and charabancs' which he ran from Tobermory and Craignure to Fionnphort, to allow a trip to Staffa and Iona. The visitors who stayed had ration coupons of their own, of course, which the hotels and boarding-houses could use to supplement their meat orders. Mr MacDougall, who had taken over the Columba in 1942, obtained a humane killing licence and had a small slaughterhouse at the back of the hotel. Five sheep per fortnight were allowed and he also killed two per week for Martha MacLeod's shop.

Holiday camps, which had begun to make an annual appearance before the war, continued to use Iona school during the holidays. Ellie Weatherhead brought the Girls' Guildry from Dundee for a number of years, for example, and groups of young men or women from the Pearce Institute in Govan also came. So there was still a hum of new activity each summer and, as ever, the visitors lent a willing hand with concerts and sports events in aid of wartime causes. A programme for a relay race has survived from those years. It was scrupulously organised with the teams, all in different colours of shirt, drawn from among the islanders, the visitors, the Iona Community ministers and RAF servicemen. There was a starter at Lagandorain gate, umpires along the route and collectors ready to accost spectators in aid of funds for Oban Cottage Hospital.

Two Canadian airmen on leave were among the visitors one summer, Charles Malcolm MacInnes and Alex MacArthur. It was an unexpected chance for them to see the birthplace of their ancestors. Charles's people had left the West End in the 1840s and Alex was a grandson of Peter MacArthur who had emigrated twice, earning his nickname of Peter the Gold in the mines of Australia and then coming back for a spell before going out to Canada with his wife, Mary MacDonald from a croft at Martyrs Bay, in 1859.

A unit of the Home Guard was formed, under the charge of Ian MacKenzie. The official look-out this time was located not at the North End but on Faradh, the high ground just to the south of the Machair. This was a better vantage point for the whole western seaboard where there was a considerable amount of convoy activity, since Oban was a convoy assembly point at the beginning of the war. Those appointed to the look-out were Captain Malcolm MacLeod, Alex MacMillan, John MacCormick Ruanaich and Dugald MacCormick Sìthean.

For most of the war, too, there was an RAF signal unit on top of Dùn I and men were billeted in Achabhaich barn. Their task was to maintain radio signals with the aircraft flying out from Oban. There was another small RAF unit at Carsaig on the south coast of Mull. Enemy mining was not a major hazard but there was always the chance of a rogue mine floating adrift, which was what brought Fingal's Cave on Staffa within a hairbreadth of serious damage in May 1945. The rock fall which resulted left a white calcinated mark on the columns just south of the cave, visible for years afterwards.

Another alarming event in the district had happened in January 1943 when the *SS Oostende*, a Belgian vessel carrying munitions, ran aground just west of Bunessan and exploded. The ceiling of a nearby cottage fell in, debris showered over a wide area and the enormous noise and flames caused near-panic in the neighbourhood, many people fleeing their homes towards Ardtun and even as far as Pennyghael. The aftermath brought a bonus, however, when it became clear that the ship had had a mixed cargo which, in the age-old way of the sea, came to rest along the coastline and met up with carts and boats homing in from all over Mull and Iona. Particularly welcome were boxes of lard and sacks of white flour, still perfectly usable after the soaked outer layer was slowly dried off to form a crust.

'S gur ann Di-luain a rinn i gluasad, am *Baron Renfrew* 's i dol a shèoladh – It was on a Monday that she set off, the *Baron Renfrew* she set sail', run the first lines of a song made by Annie Graham of Millbrae in Bunessan to mark an earlier episode, in 1941, when a Hogarth line ship called the *Baron Renfrew* had a narrow escape. A torpedo had put her engines out of action and, abandoned by the crew, she was drifting near Gometra until spotted by Johnnie Campbell on Iona who alerted the Navy at Tobermory. Before the Navy's boats could arrive, however, the *Dunara Castle* passed on her way from Tiree to Bunessan and, as a second song by John Campbell Taoslan records, 'S i an *Dunara* a shàbhail am *Baron* san àm, o na sgeirean tha millteach aig beul Loch nan Ceall – It was the *Dunara* who saved the *Baron* from the deadly rocks at the mouth of Loch na Keal'. Both songs praise Captain Clark and his crew who got a line on board the much larger vessel and towed her to safety. Back on Iona, however, merchant sea-man Neillie Betsy (Neil MacInnes) waxed indignant at a missed oppor-tunity. If only Johnnie Campbell had just told him, then he and Neil MacArthur could have gone out in a motor boat, clambered on board, dropped the anchor and sat awaiting the navy tugs plus a reward of half the salvage!

Most of the available Iona men, those not needed for essential work on the island, joined the Navy although Malcolm Black went out to Egypt with a battalion of the Argylls and Johnnie MacInnes, who was in the Kings Own Scottish Borderers when he was called up, was selected for commission and posted with a recruit party to the Argylls in Malaya. Others found their skills were required nearer home, for example Willie Coll and Angie MacKay who were joiners in the boat repair yard at Oban. Lachie Cameron worked there too as a general labourer.

Early experience in island waters sometimes stood the Iona lads in good stead. Dugald MacArthur was already on the Clyde Patrol in the first year of the war when he met one of the MacLeod boys, Malcolm. He had joined the Navy in Portsmouth where, he told Dugald, it had been announced one day that the Navy was looking for volunteers used to working in small motor boats. Having often run his father's boats, Malcolm had put himself forward – 'and the next thing was I found myself in Glasgow running the Admiral's barge!'

Bonfires flared on Dùn I and from the top of Tormore across the Sound in May 1945, when news came that the war had ended. And the community came to terms with varying news about islanders who had served in the forces. Sixteen names were added to the War Memorial at Martyrs Bay: sons, husbands, brothers, friends. John Patterson was awarded the DFC posthumously, for his many operations as wireless operator with the RAF. Among others who won distinction was Captain Donald MacDonald of the Machair family, given the George Medal for manœuvring his merchant ship clear of an attacking cruiser under a smoke screen and then returning to pick up eighty-five survivors. Charles Kirkpatrick came through, after being reported missing when the ship he was supposed to be on was sunk off West Africa. He had been taken off at the last minute to be hospitalised for malaria. But Johnnie MacInnes did not come back from Malaya. Missing there since 1942, news of his death in captivity did not reach the family in Iona until the surviving prisoners were released in August 1945.

At home, the war years also claimed several familiar figures from the older generation. Two respected sea captains died, Malcolm MacLeod in 1943 and Colin Cameron, born at Traighmòr, in 1944. Captain Cameron had commanded the *Sheila* and the *Lochinvar*, among others, during his career of over fifty years with MacBrayne's. He had been on the bridge of the *Sheila* that fateful night at the end of the First World War, when servicemen were returning to Lewis and those his ship could not carry were put on board the doomed *Iolaire*.

Among the families long connected with the land, Sergeant Donald Black Clachancorrach died in 1940, Archibald MacArthur Clachanach in 1941, Archibald Macdonald Ardionra in 1943 and John MacMillan Lagnagiogan in 1945. The last had handed over to his son only five years earlier, at which point he had been on the Duke of Argyll's rent roll for sixty-one years, longer than any other tenant on the island and the only one then still alive who had signed the petition requesting the Napier Commission to hear the tenants' complaints.

The obituary of Captain George Ritchie in 1943 began: 'It is difficult to think of Iona without the Ritchies.' Once in his own wanderings, in Australia, he had met a family who had left Iona before his own had moved in and who flatly refused to believe that anyone of that name lived there. Yet this one generation, of unusual ability and character, had indeed become fully part of the island's story and contributed much to its cultural and community life.

Anecdotes abound about George, the free-spirited mariner, who was seldom settled for long. He first crossed the Atlantic at 14 years of age, on an Allan Line clipper. In 1921 he captained the smallest craft ever to make that voyage, the 50-ton *Rockfinch*, which he sailed from the Clyde to Demerara in the West Indies in thirty-six days. The family knew George was still alive when a telegram would arrive at Iona Post Office, asking for ten pounds to be wired to some corner of the globe, perhaps to South America or to Canton where he was made a free citizen. Once he reappeared after an absence of five years, wearing an Egyptian fez. Latterly he lived in a small concrete hut, demolished after his death, close to the Sound of Iona. Salt water was surely in his veins.

Alexander and Euphemia Ritchie had died in the first weeks of 1941, within two days of each other. Their Iona Celtic Art shop within the nunnery precincts was bequeathed to the Highland Home Industries, under whose name it continued for about another twenty-five years. Jean MacDonald came over from Kentra as a girl of 14 in 1919, to work first of all in the Argyll Hotel and then for twenty very happy years as housekeeper to the Ritchies. She recalls them sketching out their craft designs in pencil, always calling her in to have a look, and the stream of visitors hospitably received at Shuna Cottage. The Ritchies loved music and so the visitors included the Kennedy Frasers and, very regularly, the artist Cadell for whom the couple had especial affection. Their Sealyham terrier Fifie was the humble subject of one of his paintings.

The Ritchies' little guidebook on the history, geology and place-names of the island was the first, in 1928, to be published by local people. To Alex Iona was one of the world's great places of pilgrimage, although that did not prevent his whimsical humour spilling over into the serious matter of guiding. The best-known story is of the visitor who quibbled about the supposed burial places of Duncan and Macbeth, apparently described as close together the previous year. Without hesitation Alex replied that their ghosts had been heard to quarrel so much over the winter that it had been necessary to separate them. An alternative version of the retort was that the islanders had little to do in the winter and so spent their time shifting the grave-slabs around. Given that the slabs had in fact been somewhat arbitrarily moved around, by nineteenth-century antiquarians, this may have been his favourite reply since it is very likely he was questioned about Macbeth's grave more than once. It remains a frequent – and unanswerable – question to this day.

On another occasion, Alex solemnly assured a group of Americans that a colony of sacred monkeys lived behind the hill. One such animal, brought back from Africa by Johnnie Wood – the schoolmaster's son – had indeed been spied swinging among the trees beside the school-house. This monkey, incidentally, had a colourful career. It caused great excitement among the local children on the day it had watched Mrs Wood kill and pluck a chicken and copied the exercise on a fellow exotic pet, an unfortunate parrot.

Alex Ritchie's first love had been the sea and a written reminiscence by a friend, who last saw him on his eightieth birthday, reflects this. As the ferry bearing the departing friend pulled away from the jetty, another boat drew in 'and Alex stepped ashore from it with lively zest, carrying a string of saithe from an early evening's fishing'.

There had been a gap in the Fionnphort to Iona ferry service when John MacDonald resigned on grounds of ill health late in 1943. The appointed successor, Angus MacKechnie from Inbhir near Kentra, was serving with the merchant navy and it took several weeks of effort by the County Council and the local MP before he could be relieved of his duties and take up the post on 1 February 1944. Neil MacArthur had filled in for most of the period, by ferrying mail and passengers in his own boat.

Leafing through John MacDonald's log book over his last eight years on the ferry reinforces awareness of the crucial link it was. The brief pencil entries record the daily to and fro of ordinary life: the movement of livestock to the Mull sales, scholars leaving for Oban, funerals and weddings, changes in the mail, the arrival and departure of minister, doctor, factor, visitors. And every day he noted the weather and the strength of the wind.

The war intruded too, beginning with the terse sentence on 31 August 1939, 'Germany invaded Poland 5.30am'. There is mention of gas masks issued a week later, of the first Air Raid Precautions lecture at Iona that November, of two seamen's bodies washed ashore the following autumn and of a mine floating through the Sound in 1942, to explode on the Black Beacon. An entry for a February day in 1942 reads 'HMS *Lady Sharazad*' but there was no fare. The one passenger was his nephew Dugald MacArthur who happened to be in the crew carrying out anti-submarine exercises between Iona, Staffa and the

Figure 16 Angus (right) and Dan MacKechnie, ferrymen on the Fionnphort to Iona service 1944–66. Photographed on Coronation Day, 1953, by visitor Bruce Ingram, brother-in-law of parish minister Revd Ewen MacLean.

Treshnish Isles. After a day ashore, Dugald was put back on board by his brother along with a bag of potatoes and a few dozen eggs.

The report of the retirement presentation to John MacDonald, in April 1944, noted that contributions had come from many parts of Scotland, England and even Canada because 'interest in the ferry to Iona and its ferryman is world wide'. This continued to be just as true in the years that followed and successor Angie MacKechnie, assisted by his brother Dan, ably inherited the task of providing a friendly face and helping hand to visitors on the last lap of their journey.

Their banter with the passengers, and between themselves, is also recalled with affection. For example, fame or status conferred no automatic privileges for this was first and foremost a local service. An exceptional crossing was made one spring Sunday in 1944 for the cast and crew at that time in Mull, making the classic film *I Know Where I'm Going*. The return from Iona was delayed while discussions continued about using one of Ian MacKenzie's boats for a particular sequence. Dugald MacArthur, at the end of his leave, and Neil, on his way to Oban, took the chance to cross with the party when it finally left. Half way over, Angie called to Dan to head for the Bull Hole anchorage, in order to show the film crew another boat, but the answer was firm: 'No, the boys have been kept back long enough, we'll just land them in Fionnphort first!'

16

The Post-War Years

In September 1949 Niall Diarmid Campbell, tenth Duke of Argyll, was buried in the family graveyard at Kilmun. He had inherited the estates from his uncle in 1914 and continued the close interest in Iona that his father, Lord Archibald Campbell, had also taken. Both of them visited regularly, getting to know the islanders personally, giving assistance with matters such as house repairs and joining in the recreation and the worship of the people.

Two generations later, however, the trustees of the tenth Duke's estate were to be faced with an insurmountable burden of accumulated death duties and in consequence, in 1979, reluctantly decided to put Iona up for sale. During those thirty years the last major inroads of the twentieth century made their mark on the island, affecting both the way its people lived and the way it was perceived by the outside world. Yet behind all the changes there still lay a few solid strands of continuity.

There was no official census in 1941 and that for 1951 showed a rise to 173 for the population of Iona. This was slightly inflated, however, by the presence of workmen and students with the Iona Community and by early visitors and hotel staff as the tourist season began to extend into the spring months. The census figures for all post-war decades in a place such as Iona have to take into account these extra, temporary numbers. The total of permanent residents since 1945 has consistently hovered around one hundred.

The school roll dipped to three or four just before the Second World

War and again in the mid-1970s, but at no time was there a real threat to the existence of the school, an indicator of any community's strength. In 1953 Mary Yuille retired after thirty-five years' teaching service in the parish, nearly twenty of them in Iona. In the log book she recorded: 'Throughout these years and at all stages the pupils have been a joy to teach.' She had begun across the Sound in Creich where her father too was a long-serving and respected headmaster. On her death she left Iona school a small legacy with which her successor, Margaret MacArthur, bought a tape recorder, record-player and barometer.

The eye of another modern gadget, the cine-camera, caught the schoolchildren dancing to a record-player in the early 1960s, in a film made by Edith Dietze ter Meer from the Black Forest in Germany. She herself had danced in the boathouse, under the swinging oil-lamps, on her first visit in 1924. Captivated by the island and, later, inspired by the work of the Iona Community she returned many times and her film was shown on German television.

For still the visitors came, from farther and farther afield, to the hotels and houses for let and to those who took boarders. New generations of regulars were created. Just after the war David Thomson, recuperating from prisoner-of-war camp, came with his brother and sister-in-law to the Argyll Hotel where they had spent their honeymoon. Mrs Willow Campbell poured cream on his porridge and generally spoiled him and so, in gratitude, he booked a return holiday the next summer. By then the ebullient Perth businessman was hooked and persuaded numbers of his friends to accompany him over many succeeding seasons. One of them, Jimmy Cairncross, agreed at first only to a long weekend in what did not sound a very exciting destination, but he too was soon a member of what became known as 'the Perth crowd'.

In those pre-licensed days their luggage was famous for clinking as it landed on the jetty, in anticipation of the congenial cocktail hours they organised in the hotel. Visitors and islanders continued to enjoy concerts and dances together, plus now also the entertainment of film nights courtesy of the Highlands and Islands Film Guild set up in 1946. In 1968, the 'Honorable Company of Iona Golfers', of which Ernest Brown and then David Thomson were the early presidents, revived the golf tournament. This keenly contested drive-and-putt around the Machair raised funds for a local cause and continues to do so, each August.

Special days and events stand out in each decade. There was a larger than usual invasion of holiday-makers, relatives and diverse dignitaries over the weekend of 12 August 1956. They were there to witness what the newspapers called the first visit to the Sacred Isle by a reigning monarch since the days of Malcolm Canmore. Queen Victoria, certainly, had not deigned to step ashore from the yacht during her 1847 cruise. But as there is no evidence that Malcolm or Margaret ever did go to Iona, and as earlier royal personages had been landed in a less than hale and hearty condition, it is quite feasible that Elizabeth was the first living monarch on the island since Colum Cille consecrated Aedán there in 574.

On Coronation Day in 1953, the parish church bell had rung out as the new Queen left Westminster Abbey, the children were given a party in the hall and a bonfire was lit on Cnoc Mòr in the evening. For the royal occasion three years later, policemen were drafted in and accommodated in the already overflowing Argyll Hotel. The ever resourceful Mrs Campbell lined them up in rows on the dining-room floor for the night.

Flags and bunting fluttered and crowds, not in the least unruly, thronged the head of the jetty as Sir Charles Maclean of Duart, lord-lieutenant of Argyll, welcomed the royal party ashore. From there they walked to the cathedral to attend Sunday morning service. Several press photographers snapped the Queen, accompanied by the Revd Charles Warr of the cathedral trustees, contemplating the tombs in the Reilig Odhráin where a few of her predecessors had ended their final journey.

'Modern Miracle in Iona' proclaimed the front page of the *Weekly Scotsman* above its account of 19 September 1957. That was another memorable day, the day of 'the switch-on'. The official party, 120 strong, arrived by the *Lochfyne* and was led from the jetty by Hector Maclean, piper to Sir Charles Maclean of Duart. The children had a half-holiday and everyone crowded into the hall to see Mrs Walter Elliott, wife of the Lord High Commissioner, pull a lever to inaugurate the electricity supply from a small hydro and diesel station in

Tobermory. Behind the platform, a Celtic cross, silhouetted against a map of Iona, lit up.

Nearly half the island households, including the school, became the North of Scotland Hydro-Electric Board's newest consumers. Also present was Tom Johnston, chairman of the Board and the man above all others whose effort and vision had brought it into being. In the past eight years, he said, over one hundred thousand rural households had already been connected. Bringing light and power to the islands and glens was, in his view, an effective counter-attack on the social and economic decline of the Highlands.

There had been several small electricity generators on Iona but here now was a permanent source. A magic wand had indeed been waved, power cuts permitting of course. Archie MacDonald told a reporter that he hoped shortly to own the first television set on the island. The first paraffin refrigerator, at Cùlbhuirg, could now be superseded by more up-to-date models. A further domestic boon followed in 1959 when Loch Staonaig was made into a public reservoir.

June 1963 brought the 1400th anniversary of the coming of St Columba to Scotland and bright sunshine reigned over ten days of celebrations. On 2 June, Pentecost Sunday, the communion service was conducted by the Moderator of the Church of Scotland and by a Scots Presbyterian minister who was also a bishop of the Church of South India. In the congregation were representatives from at least half a dozen denominations and from several different countries. Viewers across Europe shared in the worship, televised live. Fittingly for this commemoration of the Columban legacy, an afternoon service in Gaelic was led by two ministers from the Presbytery of Mull, assisted by a Gaelic choir from Oban and Mull.

St Columba's Day, 9 June, fell on the following Sunday when the parish minister, the Revd David Stiven, preached at the morning service of communion. In the afternoon a vast assembly of over a thousand took part in an open-air service of commitment led by the Revd George MacLeod, and in the evening the preacher was a former moderator of the Presbyterian Church in Ireland. Links with Ireland were again underlined on 12 June, when leaders and hundreds of members of the Episcopal Church in Scotland were joined by Irish and English bishops and by over 800 pilgrims who came by chartered steamer direct from Belfast. The Archbishop of Canterbury was among those who welcomed ashore twelve men, who had rowed from Derry in a modern replica of a sixth-century curragh. The crew, robed in brown and with their oars on their shoulders, headed a colourful procession to a service in the cathedral.

Nor was Colum Cille forgotten elsewhere in the Gaidhealtachd. At Southend in Kintyre there was an ecumenical service in the open air, near the strange footprints in stone which mark the spot traditionally held to be where the saint first landed on mainland Scotland. This annual Conventicle, as it is known, was addressed in 1963 by Dr Leonard Small, minister of St Cuthbert's in Edinburgh and a regular visitor to Iona. On Canna, Mass was celebrated in the church followed by a Benediction on the green field of Keill, where an early church dedicated to the saint once resounded with praise and where a fine carved cross still stands. Over eighty people attended, from all the Small Isles and from the mainland. The service was the idea of John Lorne Campbell, then owner of the island, and his wife Margaret Fay Shaw. In her autobiography years later, she was to record her pleasure at being told by people, long afterwards, that they had been on Canna for St Columba's Day and they would never forget it.

In June 1965 there was another service of thanksgiving on Iona, attended by people from all over the world. This was to mark the end of the rebuilding programme, and the honour of opening the door to the newly completed West Range fell appropriately to David Russell, whose father and family had done so much to support the work of the Iona Cathedral Trust and the Iona Community. The restoration of the buildings was a considerable achievement. The Community's indefatigable leader had coaxed the money out of institutions and individuals at home and abroad, through a combination of personal charisma and very hard work.

Tensions on the island itself had eased since the first difficult years and the Revd Ewen MacLean – who came to the parish charge in 1947 and was also its last Gaelic-speaking minister – established a good working relationship with the Revd George MacLeod which his successors inherited. Parish services continued to be held in the cathedral in summer. Ewen MacLean recalls that a sign of the new season was when Hector MacNiven came with his horse and cart to transfer the

Figure 17   Revd Ewen MacLean, soon after becoming parish minister of
Iona in 1947, with members of the Kirk Session: (left to right) Hector
MacNiven, John Campbell, Peter MacInnes, Duncan MacArthur and John
MacCormick. Photograph courtesy of Ewen MacLean.

'kist o'whistles', the small pedal organ, from the church up the road to
the cathedral nave. Ministers from the Iona Community helped to fill
in during periods of vacancy or holiday absence in the parish. A few
were particularly good at building bridges with the local people and
among those usually credited with this quiet background work were
Cameron Wallace and Hamish MacIntyre. The carpenters and masons
employed by the Community in the early 1950s were joined by a number of men from the Ross of Mull, for example Calum MacPherson,
Clerk of Works, Hugh Lamont and his son (also Hugh), Johnnie 'na
Creig' Campbell and Attie MacKechnie. The piping and singing talents
of several of them were welcome additions to island concerts during
their years on the rebuilding team.

    Nevertheless, in no way could it be claimed that 'a common life with
the Community of Iona' had been achieved, the aim wistfully aired in
the first issue of *The Coracle* more than a quarter of a century before.

Neither the practical nor the spiritual vision of George MacLeod had been rooted at the start within the local community and the development of the Iona Community over the years had taken a course largely parallel to life on the island. In fact, it had become an island within an island. And this dual identity was to become even more marked beyond the milestone of 1965, when the Community had to evolve a new programme of activity, both in the residential buildings on Iona which they now occupied with the permission of the cathedral trustees, and on the mainland. It was this lively, often controversial, movement within the Church of Scotland that was to become more and more identified in the public mind with the place whose name it had taken. Indeed, the place and its people came near, at times, to total eclipse.

The nunnery remained as it was. Back in 1948 George MacLeod had turned 'wondering eyes' towards it and briefly contemplated the possibility of a summer hostel for young people there. There were later proposals, in the 1950s and the 1970s, to rebuild the ruins but nothing came of these. Many people enjoy the quiet atmosphere of the nunnery cloisters and even prefer them, it must be said, to the restored but busy buildings up the road.

The crofting part of the island's economy continued to revolve around the raising and selling of sheep and cattle. There was a scare in 1952, following an outbreak of foot-and-mouth disease in the Ross of Mull. As a precaution, passengers and any stock being transported had to wade through disinfected straw on arrival in Iona and, fortunately, the epidemic was contained. Data collected in 1947 by Frank Fraser Darling for his comprehensive work on Highland land use, the *West Highland Survey*, provide a snapshot of crofting practice on the island in the immediate post-war years. Manure, seaweed and shell sand were spread on the fields which bore crops, in rotation, of oats, barley, hay, potatoes or turnips. Oats had not always done so well on their own and a mixture of small oats and rye was sometimes sown. Blackface ewes were commonly crossed with Leicester tups and the cattle were bred from a Highland or shorthorn bull provided, one to each township, by the Department of Agriculture. The crofters reared their own calves to replace the stock.

The sailors on the *Dunara Castle* used to say that the fields of Iona were the first to turn yellow-green in spring. It was a sign of the new season, as they steamed north among the islands their vessel served. In his survey, Fraser Darling described Iona as 'extraordinarily green and fertile', partly owing to the continuance of traditional practice in preparing the arable ground and the presence of cattle, good for keeping down endemic problems such as thistles. The proportion of sheep to cattle had increased enormously over the century, however. Compared to the 1890s, when they had been about equal on each holding, Department of Agriculture figures quoted in the *Third Statistical Account* of 1955 showed the difference. Across the island there were 181 cattle, mostly beef, as against 1,530 sheep. There were still 12 horses in total and poultry on most crofts.

A lot of work was still done communally, gathering sheep from the hill pasture, clipping and dipping at the fanks in Calva and on the Machair. Sheep were also put out on to off-lying islands, such as Rèidhlean which went with Calva, or Soa which was shared by the West End tenants. Dugald MacArthur remembers his father's boat being used regularly to take twenty to thirty sheep to Soa in the spring and bring them back in the autumn. The grazing was good there and sorrel grew well. Once, in the 1950s, he took the crofters out for the clipping, often a tricky task once the animals had adapted to freedom from human interference for several months. Most of the sheep were gathered into one spot but two remained very elusive:

> The idea was to drive them down to the rocky side and corner them there, but they got stuck out on a point at the east end ... so I had to go right round and edge in – luckily it was calm – and land Dougie Black and Peter MacInnes and Jimmy Beaton, who caught the sheep and clipped them there and then on the rocks. They got the fleeces in and left the sheep, it was important to get the wool away with the rest.

Veterinary help had long been found among the islanders themselves. Hector MacNiven at Maol, for example, was expert at diagnosing a problem or performing an operation if necessary. His father Neil had been widely known in the district for his skill in the tending of sick animals, learned partly from books and a good deal from experience.

Figure 18 Clipping sheep on Soa, 1950. Peter MacInnes and Dugald Black are in the boat, in the foreground. Photographed by Dugald MacArthur.

After Hector retired, Peter MacInnes was often called upon, as was Hector's nephew Neil MacArthur who had inherited much of the same expertise.

Tarmac gradually replaced the gravel surface of the island's mile or

Figure 19   Neil MacArthur, ploughing below Clachanach 1944.

so of public road, as the horse and cart gave way to motor vehicles.
Walter Tindal at the Columba had the first tractor in the early 1950s, a
thirsty petrol guzzler. A model run on a more economical mixture of
petrol and paraffin was the next to arrive, at Sìthean, and Clachanach
then brought in the first diesel tractor. Horses were phased out gradually and were still swum across the Sound up to the end of the decade.
The last working horse, belonging to Johnnie Dougall at Ardionra, was
put out to graze the East End hills in retirement in 1961.

The perennial question of a reliable means of transporting goods and
livestock arose again when MacBrayne discontinued several cargo
steamer services in 1962, including that to Iona. Freight now had to be
landed at Tobermory and conveyed across Mull, a less than satisfactory
alternative. A measure of improvement came over the next few years
when the new pier was built at Craignure and the road upgraded
between there and Fionnphort. With the arrival of the *Columba* on the
Oban–Mull run in 1964, cars and lorries need no longer be swung
precariously on to the deck, but simply driven on board. Welcoming
the car-ferry era, the Revd David Stiven wrote in his newsletter: 'How

fitting it is that a ship with such a name – and for such a purpose – should be under the command of an Iona man. May Captain Colin MacDonald infect all his passengers with something of his own happiness!'

Dr Stiven's first Christmas present to himself when he came to the Iona manse in 1958 was a duplicating machine. With commendable energy every month he typed and cranked out *Cell and Coracle*, two pages full of lively parish news, both clerical and secular. This was Dr Stiven's last charge. He loved talking with the old folk and had a kindly rapport too with the young. And he came to know what affected the lives of the people in Mull and Iona and aroused their sympathies, as when he recorded the tragic loss with all hands of the old *Lochinvar* off Humberside on 2 April 1966. For half a century she had plied the Sound of Mull, part of the lifeline to the mainland for both islands.

On 16 September 1974, the *King George V* sailed to Staffa and Iona for the last time. She had been a familiar sight on the horizon each season for nearly forty years and was held in much affection, although the islanders had vigorously objected to the extension of her timetable to Sundays, in 1971. And with her departure came an end to the local use of the red boats and their crews, featured in countless holiday photographs and postcards as they ferried passengers, luggage and mailbags ashore. Those last in charge were Archie MacDonald on the *Ulva*, Bob MacLelland on the *Applecross* and Doodie MacFadyen on the *Iona*. Each employed a man at the bow and, very often, a youngster on board to hold the rope in the coveted position of stern-boy.

Day trips direct from Oban were later reinstated with a twice-weekly service in summer, using the *Columba* and the Iona ferry as tender, but this too eventually came to an end on grounds of economy. It was as if the arteries of the Hebrides, along which had teemed coracle and galley, smack and schooner and steamship, were finally shrinking. After many centuries of use, the seaways seemed to be drying up, at least amid the mountains of paper on planning officials' desks.

So virtually everything and everybody would be channelled through Oban and over Mull. But they would reach their destination more efficiently, via the new terminals and vehicular vessel between Fionnphort and Iona. Notice of this proposal was made public by Argyll County

a

b

c

Figure 20 (*a*) Charlie Kirkpatrick, baiting lines, 1939. Photograph courtesy of Elizabeth McFadzean.　(*b*) Donald MacFadyen, 'Doodie', at the helm of his red boat, waiting to take steamer passengers ashore at Staffa, 1960s. Photograph courtesy of Jane MacFadyen.　(*c*) Archibald MacArthur at the tiller, 1940.

Council on 30 November 1972. The previous month, MacBrayne, now in public ownership as Caledonian MacBrayne, had taken over the ferry service. Alistair Gibson, who had succeeded the MacKechnies on their retirement in 1966, was the last private operator across the Sound of Iona.

The Council received a stream of objections, many from visitors to Iona, alarmed that the plans would mean unlimited traffic and an end to the island's peaceful charm. At the local inquiry held in Bunessan in December 1973, however, it was made clear that it had never been the intention to permit tourists' cars or caravans to use the ferry. The islanders' concerns, on the whole, focused on the practicalities of their year-round needs. They had earlier pressed for a deep-water pier, to allow puffers and small cargo vessels to come alongside. Indeed, as far back as 1930 they had lobbied the County Council with precisely that end in view and there had been talk of using Rudh na h-Aird, north of the present jetty, as the site. But the proposal had always been rejected as too costly. The District Councillor from Iona, Peter MacInnes, stated at the inquiry that what the local community was now seeking was a ferry service as safe, convenient and flexible as possible for both goods and passengers.

Construction of the terminals began in 1977 and the *MV Morvern* made the first run, with Donald MacNeill from Colonsay on the bridge, in May 1979. Seton Gordon would have found this type of broad, bow-ramped vessel even less photogenic than the motor boats he was regretful to see oust the sail more than fifty years before. It has been likened to an animated biscuit tin. But fuel, equipment, feedstuff and livestock could now be transported door to door and for a crofting island this was of very considerable benefit. Medical help too would now be swifter. Early that summer, the Mull and Iona ambulance crossed for the first time, to attend to a cyclist injured outside the school.

The last day of February 1979 brought Iona into the headlines yet again. Nearly three centuries of ownership by the House of Argyll was signalled to be drawing to an end when the trustees of the Argyll Estates, of which the twelfth Duke was a member, announced that their land in Iona and the Ross of Mull was to be sold. The need to

meet death duties still outstanding on the tenth Duke's estate had
eventually, though regretfully, forced this decision.

The properties were not to be placed formally on the market until
May but, in the interim, there was a tidal wave of media attention and
press correspondence. Recurring themes were that the sale might
threaten the island's peace, the memory of St Columba and, above all,
our 'heritage', described variously as glorious or sacred and usually as
national. Questions of farm rents and local amenities received some
comment but not a great deal. Only a very few drew attention to the
people of the Ross of Mull, also facing uncertainty until a new landlord
came forward. In the end, that part of the estate was not sold. Meanwhile, enquiries flowed into the estate agent's office from all over the
country and the world.

The Duke went on record as agreeing with public sentiment that
Iona should only go to a buyer prepared 'to maintain its unique
character'. On two occasions he received the entire Iona Community
Council and listened carefully to their concerns. When Community
Councils were created in the mid-1970s, the proposal was for one body
representing Mull and Iona jointly. The islanders had argued successfully, however, that two separate councils would better serve their
sometimes shared, but often distinctive, needs. This was undoubtedly
one such occasion. Many of the islanders were genuinely sorry to lose
their Argyll landlords, with whom relationships in recent generations
had been amicable and untroubled. Some who worked the land felt
that transfer of ownership to the Department of Agriculture would be
the most appropriate option for a crofting and farming community.

On 24 May, two days after the official opening date, an offer of one
and a half million pounds from the Fraser Foundation was accepted.
Sir Hugh Fraser stated that Iona had been bought for the nation as a
memorial to his father, the late Lord Fraser of Allander. Adminis-
tration of the property was placed initially in the hands of the Secretary
of State for Scotland until it was announced, in late December, that the
island would pass into the care of the National Trust for Scotland.

An early bid by the National Trust to buy Iona outright had been
unsuccessful. It had, however, kept up a public appeal all summer
which, after talks with the Iona Cathedral Trust, was reoriented
towards a joint effort to raise funds for much needed maintenance

work on the fabric of the ecclesiastical buildings. This led directly to the setting-up of a small permanent workforce to look after the historic sites and their grounds. The many individuals, groups and churches who had dug into their pockets 'to save Iona' thus saw their contributions put to practical use, helping preserve that aspect of the island which, almost certainly, was of most interest to them.

Although a photograph of the cathedral featured regularly in the worldwide publicity surrounding the sale, neither it nor the Reilig Odhráin or the nunnery were affected. These continued to be the responsibility of the cathedral trustees. Designations of several ancient monuments and a conservation area, covering the entire village and part of the adjacent farms, remained in place and much of the agricultural land was still under crofting tenure.

In practical terms, not a great deal had changed. Yet a sum of well over a million pounds had been spent. What exactly, one cannot help wondering, had been for sale?

Part Four

Bidh I mar a bha
Iona shall be as it was

17

Postscript

An I mo chridhe, I mo ghràidh
An àite guth manaich bidh geum bà
Ach mun tig an saoghal gu crìch
Bidh I mar a bha.

Since at least the late eighteenth century, the old saying about cattle
lowing where once monks sang has been the subject of conjecture.
At various stages, claims have been advanced that the fulfilment of the
prophecy was drawing nigh: when the ruins were first enclosed, when
a new parish church and manse were built, when the cathedral church
was restored. It has been particularly identified with the Iona Community and its achievement in completing the monastic complex adjacent to the church in the course of this century. Before the world shall
come to an end, Iona shall be as it was.

Some of this has always seemed to me a little curious since, if the
words did belong to St Columba, it is hardly likely he was referring to
the renovation of a Benedictine settlement founded more than six
hundred years after his own death. To be fair, George MacLeod always
stressed that the physical rebuilding was also a symbol for the more
important task of bringing work and worship back together, an idea he
believed was central to the early Celtic church. There is a parallel too
between the activities of the Iona Community on the mainland, and
elsewhere in the world, and the missionary role which Iona undoubtedly once had.

It is the literal interpretation of the prophecy, however, that is implied, without further question, time and again. Since we do not know for certain who said it or what was actually meant, is there not scope for more imaginative flights of fancy? The sentiments could even be those of an early green soothsayer, gloomily forecasting that we will be left again with bare rocks and ocean if we do not treat the ecological systems of the planet with more care ...

Whatever Iona once was, the public assumption of what it now is always strikes me as a little narrow. A skim through the stack of newspaper cuttings relating to the sale of the island in 1979 reinforces this impression. I do not have a ready answer to the question at the end of the previous chapter, and raising it is not intended to detract from the generosity of the Fraser Foundation's gesture, nor from the genuine concern expressed by many members of the public. But setting aside the absurd situation whereby tracts of land command price-tags way beyond their economic value – an all too familiar event in the Highlands anyway – the intense interest reflected the fact that for many Iona is primarily, even solely, a site of historic and religious significance. Thus, in a sense, it is also seen as a piece of public property.

It is not hard to see how this has happened. The late Professor Douglas Young of St Andrews University took an invigorating gallop through the country's religious history in his book *Scotland*. For most of us, he pointed out, our notions of the past are a midden-heap of half-remembered school lessons, the odd historical novel and a few colourful incidents regurgitated regularly for the benefit of tourists. More or less at the start was St Columba, 'merely the most permanently influential of a series of hot-gospelling Irish revivalists', then there were St Margaret, John Knox, Jenny Geddes, the Covenanters and so on. And nowadays there was George MacLeod and his Iona Community, 'which must have something to do with that vague St Columba' away at the beginning. The story thus becomes telescoped. Only a couple of striking images, out of a long and complex picture, stick in the popular imagination.

Yet there are always other ways of looking at a place, even one as famous as Iona, and there are good reasons for going there that have nothing to do with saintly figures from any century. Artists have long been drawn to it, as Chapter 12 describes. Geologists consider it of very great interest and botanists find in its range of typically Hebridean habitats a rich, relatively undisturbed flora. And very large numbers, over a very long time, have visited often as a result of family and friendship links. I had no idea that the island where our summer holidays were spent was in the least bit special to anyone else, until St Columba featured in a primary school class. It was above all where a grandmother lived, a sturdy figure in long black skirt and purple shawl whom I can see yet making her dignified way ahead of us towards the cathedral for the parish service or thrashing at thistles with a walking stick or, up to the elbows in flour and battered baking tins, exhorting us to be sure and eat plenty.

I do know people who have been profoundly affected by a visit to the island, who have experienced there a sense of peace and sanctity. Some have been only once, many have returned. There is a proverb, indeed, which claims that the person who goes to Iona will go there three times – am fear a thèid a dh'I, thèid e trì uairean ann. But beware, for within it lurks a pun. In Gaelic it can also sound as if they who go to utter destruction will do so three times!

For I have to say that I have also met people who are disappointed by Iona, who find nothing particularly special about the atmosphere. Is this partly because of overblown expectations? When it has been described as 'a major planetary centre of spiritual power', for example, where the very rocks speak, then the reality may well fall short of the advance reputation. And if these mystical qualities are so obvious, why have I never felt them, coming from a family who has lived for several generations amid the self-same landscape? Perhaps I am not in tune, possibly my approach is too prosaic. What is a druidic temple to some is a sheep-fank to me. Sorry about that. There again, as I have argued, such spots might have served both purposes, although I maintain strong reservations about what we can possibly assume the Druids actually thought and did.

I have certainly often found the spirits refreshed on Iona, the mind eased. There can be days of breathless calm, when the grey stillness is almost tangible and you think that even the grass must have stopped growing. But I have felt very much the same in other places with that mixture of rock and turf, sea and sky – in the Ross of Mull just over the Sound, on Tiree or on Eriskay, which is remarkably reminiscent of Iona.

Figure 21   Bringing a horse ashore at Iona, after swimming it from Mull, early 1950s. The horse's owner, Neil MacArthur, is behind Angie MacKay in the stern; Jimmy Beaton and Johnnie MacFarlane are at the oars; Willie MacDonald is in the bow.

There *is* something distinctive and magnetic about the Hebridean landscape in general. And it is special too because for so long, although not always without difficulty, it has sustained communities of people. I pondered these things once, under the broad skies of Lewis, standing at the house in Ness where my maternal grandfather was born. A Gaelic-speaker, of gentle manner and kindly brown eyes, he spent most of his adult life as a schoolmaster in Argyll. But he had been brought up on a croft, at approximately the same time my Iona grandfather was growing up on his, yet there were definite differences. Here in Ness was a mere pocket handkerchief of grassland, sloping down to the blue Atlantic. No stretch of good hill pasture led away from the back of the house. His people had been pushed out here, two generations before, when the township of Capadal was one of several cleared from the fertile swathe of land around Uig Bay on the west of the island.

Crofting communities have a great deal in common but their origins and development have varied much from place to place. This book and its predecessor have attempted not only to bring the local population of Iona out of the shadows, but also to show that their history has had its own particular character, its own twists and turns along the way. Some might consider that this has been a parochial exercise. A devotee of the island once said to me that 'Iona is for the whole world', such is its spiritual prestige. I have to respect that view but would simply add this: if you study any locality, however small, and try to write about it with clarity and integrity, then you are illustrating human experience and touching on human values that are universal. And so in that sense Iona's local history too is 'for the world'.

During the outcry over the sale of Iona, the impression was that rather more of it came from the leafy suburbs of the cities than, say, from the crofting townships of the Outer Isles. There are fewer people there now, of course, even fewer than last century when Alexander Carmichael gleaned his remnants of traditional lore which still included many invocations to Iona's saint. Had there been a similar clamour back in 1879 to 'save for the nation' the Gaelic language, and the economic base of the communities where Gaels lived, then more of them might have been around to add a word of support, in the language Colum Cille himself spoke.

This brings me to a paradox touched upon in Chapter 14, about the arrival of the Iona Community. Its late founder, and its ongoing work, have built up a committed following all over the world. Yet in no fundamental sense at all is it rooted in the Gaelic heartland of Scotland. A few individuals of Highland background, or who were Gaelic-speakers, have been involved over the years but in nothing like the proportion one might expect in a movement that takes its name, and claims its inspiration, from a place whose history is intrinsic to that of Gaeldom. Indeed, it is by no means disrespectful to suggest that the Community may all along have had the wrong name. Something that expressed *what* it was trying to do, rather than where, might have avoided much misunderstanding over the years.

A few years ago, on two separate occasions, colleagues of my acquaintance enquired why neither a Gaelic Bible nor bilingual

Gaelic/English signs were in evidence within the cathedral. The Community, it is only fair to point out, does not bear overall responsibility for information boards and notices. But to reply that St Columba spoke Latin is hardly to address the point. So he did, in addition to Gaelic, but he did not speak English. Nor is it enough to take refuge in the form of liturgy which the Community has evolved, asserting that it mirrors the ethos of the early Celtic church. How can anyone be so sure? The person of Colum Cille is hard enough to flesh out, fourteen centuries down the line. We know virtually nothing about how the ordinary men and women of his time and later actually worshipped. There is a huge gulf, in terms of time and potential influences, between the Columban period and the earliest prayers that found their way, in some shape or form, into Carmichael's *Carmina Gadelica*. It is curious, by the way, that this work is often given the general label of 'Celtic' even though it is drawn from a specifically Scottish Gaelic source.

But then there has been, for a decade or so now, a positive frenzy for all things 'Celtic'. Bookshelves groan with publications full of twirly designs, gentle mysticism, green and pleasant thoughts. Donald Meek, professor of Celtic at Aberdeen University, who has written perceptively about the recent explosion in this type of literature, points out that it seldom refers to certain less kindly characteristics of the Celtic monks: their zeal for cursing another to death, for going to war, for drawing up rules of penance that were harsh in the extreme. Some of the new school of writing springs from a genuine, and quite understandable, desire to seek a counter-balance to an increasingly material and polluted world. And some of it does try to place its sources in a proper historical context. But Professor Meek stresses one crucial point. If we really wish to know how the Celts felt and behaved towards the world around them, then there has to be fresh, rigorous and scholarly analysis of such primary Irish and Scottish texts that exist, and this has to be done through their languages of origin.

For the tendency to ignore the importance of the language goes back a long way. The ensnaring of Iona into a dreamy Celtic twilight was achieved most effectively by William Sharp, whose writings under the pen-name of Fiona MacLeod began to appear in the late 1890s. I would love to have followed him around in 1894, when he visited the island. Who did he talk to and what exactly was he told? The local population were nearly all native Gaelic-speakers at that time and although Sharp may have had a few words, he was not fluent – a point made in some trenchant criticism of his literary extravagances in an *Oban Times* review around the turn of the century.

Sharp wrote of Iona: 'All the story of the Gael is here. Iona is the microcosm of the Gaelic world.' Yet he dismissed as 'accidental' the story of its acreage, fisheries and pasture, the way of life of those very Gaels with whom he spoke. And do those who acclaim him as a true exponent of the Celtic spirit realise that Sharp believed strongly that the Celtic languages themselves did not matter? He was happy to grasp what he could from their lore, reinterpret it in his own tongue and argue for a Celtic movement that was 'not partisan but content to participate in the English tradition.' He would be well pleased today.

On Là Chaluim-Chille, in Derry, people wear oak leaves in their lapels to remember Columba on his day, 9 June. He is honoured as one of the three great saints of Ireland, along with Patrick and Brigit. Across the water, on the tip of the Kintyre peninsula, the Conventicle still brings an ecumenical congregation together beside St Columba's footprints every year. On 9 June, too, the associate members of the Iona Community renew their vows, wherever they live up and down the country, and the Community's daily service on the island marks the occasion in some aspect of its worship.

All this is as it should be. The many patterns of romantic fancy woven around St Columba and his legacy ought not to obscure the fact that he remains a figure of great significance in the story of Scotland. On Iona itself he may not command the spiritual role he once did but there have been faint traces of continuity right down the ages none the less. People still work the land and to some extent the sea. Succeeding communities have in turn inherited these same resources and several families today could trace a link back to the eighteenth century at least. Only in the last seventy, out of fourteen hundred, years has the English language come to predominate over Gaelic.

Much of course is not as it was, even from the earliest years I can remember myself. A simple fishing trip has a ring of nostalgia about it now, since the coastal waters have become so depleted. One of childhood's joys was going out on a summer night to the haddie banks between Staffa and Mull and slipping home through the quiet darkness of the Sound, to a cup of tea by the yellow light of the oil-lamp while the fish were gutted ready for breakfast. In September 1962 an islander, Bobby Grey, spent such an evening off the south end of the island and wrote to my father: 'I had a lovely night's fishing with Willie Coll about ten days ago. At Sgeir an Oir. Lythe, mackerel and bodach ruadh on the spinner. Quite a night out.'

Bobby Grey's letter had been mainly about a find during excavations that summer which fascinated him greatly. A cross-slab was uncovered bearing a Norse runic inscription that read: 'Kali son of Olvir laid this stone over Fugl his brother'. It was thought to date from about the eleventh century when for some reason, for a trading mission or as a settler, Kali stayed on Iona long enough to labour over this poignant commemoration to a dead brother. If one day another was made for him, it has not been identified.

Nor, of course, will we ever know the names and resting-places of the vast majority of the people who have lived on the island. The Reilig Odhráin remains a site of solemn antiquity, a reminder of the early kingdom of Dál Riata and the once mighty Lordship of the Isles. Today, the graveyard is primarily a place of local and personal remembrance, its stones a dignified record of the close-knit and resilient community of the last two hundred years. The people have continued to gather there in mutual support, as the generations move on or are unexpectedly and cruelly interrupted. The ordinary cycle of life and death is no different on the Sacred Isle.

Out across the island unknown inhabitants long gone have left one enduring memorial to their existence, the large number of places which they named. As there is no reason to suppose the island was unoccupied at any time from at least the sixth century and probably before, then some of these names could be very old indeed. For place-names are carried through daily language and reflect the way of life. The true custodians of Iona may well be the people who, over the centuries, have bequeathed to its hills and rocks and fields the names these still bear.

The vast majority are of Gaelic origin and an intriguing number contain personal names. I often wonder who they were, especially the women – who have always contributed equally to the work of the land yet who seldom emerge from the pages of documented history. Who tilled the ground at Fang Mary, a green haven on the south-facing slopes of Dùn I? Who was Marsali, whose enclosure lies behind the village street? And did 'little Ann of the poison' actually live in the cave carved neatly out of a hillside on the Machair and long known as Uamh Anna Bhig a' Phuinsean?

The rocks of the north coast are moulded into weird and wonderful shapes, buffers between land and sea. Whether they will indeed swim above the ocean at some last cataclysmic moment, as the saying predicts, I do not know, but there is a reassuring permanence about them all the same. I walked the Calva shore there one blustery December day, as the old year blew itself out. A few seabirds, sanderlings perhaps, darted nimbly along the wave line, the foam hissing back and forth around their shanks. A curtain of spray hung over Geodha Ruairidh, the creek where Ruairidh Cameron drowned. It would have been a day like this when his small boat was swept on to these reefs one hundred and fifty years ago.

A few hundred metres out to sea Finlay's Rock turned the breakers white, as it must have done sometime in 1834 when a ship struck and was lost. Dishes of all kinds washed up on the beach, their voyage broken off for ever. Flora MacArthur, my grandmother twice great, had her son Dugald in her arms when someone picked up an ashet, patterned with small red flowers, and gave it to her for the boy. An aunt passed it on to me and I have it yet.

Flotsam and jetsam of all kinds have come my way during the course of piecing together the stories that have converged on Iona, to shape what we know of its history. That history has been made by people and interpreted by people. Without a doubt, visitors will continue to seek out the island for a variety of different reasons and they will take away from it a wide range of impressions. It is a small place to carry such a burden of history and legend, of beliefs and expectation, and we should all perhaps tread lightly. The lives played out there have indeed been extraordinary, a few of them at least. Countless others, while less remarkable and little celebrated in the public eye, have been every bit as real. All that many people have wished is that these too be remembered.

Bibliography

MAP

Recommended is *Iona: a Map*, printed by John Bartholomew & Son and published by the Iona Community (1983). It has excellent coverage of the place-names, in Gaelic and English; it includes a geological map and close-ups of the cathedral buildings and village area.

THE MONUMENTS

Royal Commission on the Ancient and Historical Monuments of Scotland (RCAHMS), *Argyll: An Inventory of the Monuments*, vol. 4: *Iona* (Edinburgh, 1982). This is the most comprehensive work to date. RCAHMS has also produced a useful booklet covering the principal sites of historic interest: *Iona* (Edinburgh, 1983, new edn 1995).

Drummond, James, *Sculptured Monuments in Iona and the West Highlands* (Edinburgh, 1881).

Graham, Henry D., *Antiquities of Iona* (London, 1850).

Steer, K. A. and Bannerman, J. W., *Late Medieval Monumental Sculpture in the West Highlands* (Edinburgh, 1977).

SELECTED PUBLISHED SOURCES

Anderson, A. O., *Scottish Annals from English Chroniclers 500 to 1286* (Stamford, 1991). First published 1908.

Anderson, A. O. and Anderson, M. O. (eds), *Adomnán's Life of Columba* (London, 1961).

Anderson, A. O. and Anderson, M. O. (eds), *Early Sources of Scottish History 500 to 1286*, 2 vols (Stamford, 1990). First published 1922.

Anderson, M. O., *Kings and Kingship in Early Scotland*, rev. edn (Edinburgh, 1980).

Bannerman, J., 'Comarba Coluim Chille and the Relics of Columba', in *The Innes Review*, vol. XLIV, no. 1 (spring 1993), pp. 14–47.

Campbell, Dr J. L., *Canna: The Story of a Hebridean Island* (Oxford, 1984).

Carmichael, Alexander, *Carmina Gadelica*, vol. I (Edinburgh, 1928), vol. II (Edinburgh, 1928), vol. III (Edinburgh, 1940), vol. IV (Edinburgh, 1941), vol. V (Edinburgh, 1954), vol. VI (Edinburgh, 1971). See also English edn (Edinburgh, 1992), in particular the Preface by John MacInnes, pp. 7–18.

Cowan, I. B. and Easson, D. E., *Medieval Religious Houses Scotland* (London and New York, 1957).

Cregeen, Eric R. (ed.), *Inhabitants of the Argyll Estate 1779* (Edinburgh, 1963).

Cregeen, Eric R. (ed.), *Argyll Estate Instructions: Mull, Morvern, Tiree 1771–1805*, Scottish History Society, fourth ser., vol. I (Edinburgh, 1964).

Dilworth, Mark, 'Iona Abbey and the Reformation' in *Scottish Gaelic Studies*, vol. 12 (1971), pp. 77–109.

Dunlop, A. I. (ed.), *Calendar of Scottish Supplications to Rome 1423–1428*, Scottish History Society, third ser., vol. XLVIII (Edinburgh, 1956).

Dunlop, A. I. (ed.), *Calendar of Scottish Supplications to Rome 1433–1447* (Glasgow, 1983).

Ferguson, Ronald, *Chasing the Wild Goose* (London, 1988).

Ferguson, Ronald, *George MacLeod* (London, 1990).

Giblin, Cathaldus (ed.), *The Irish Franciscan Mission to Scotland, 1619–1646* (Dublin, 1964).

Gordon, Seton, *Highways and Byways in the West Highlands* (London, 1935).

Herbert, Máire, *Iona, Kells and Derry: The History and Hagiography of the Monastic Familia of Columba* (Oxford, 1988).

Iona Club (eds), *Collectanea de Rebus Albanicis* (Edinburgh, 1847).

Johnson, Dr Samuel, *A Journey to the Western Islands of Scotland (1773)*, 1st edn (London, 1775).

Lamont, Angus, *Description of the Island of Iona or Icolmkill*, manuscript written in 1848, copy in possession of author.

Lindsay, E. R. and Cameron, A. I. (eds), *Calendar of Scottish Supplications to Rome 1418–1422*, Scottish History Society, third ser., vol. XXIII (Edinburgh, 1934).

Lynch, Michael, *Scotland: A New History* (London, 1991).

MacArthur, E. Mairi, *Iona: The Living Memory of a Crofting Community 1750–1914* (Edinburgh, 1990).

MacArthur, E. Mairi (ed.), *That Illustrious Island ... Iona through Travellers Eyes* (Iona, 1991).

MacBain, A. and Kennedy, J. (eds), *Reliquiae Celticae*, vol. II (includes translation of the *Book of Clanranald*) (Inverness, 1894).

MacCormick, Iain, *The Celtic Art of Iona: Drawings from the Manuscripts of the Late Alex Ritchie* (Iona, 1994).

MacDonald, A. D. S., 'Aspects of the Monastery and Monastic Life in Adomnán's Life of Columba' in *Peritia*, vol. 3 (1984), pp. 271–302.

MacDonald, Revd Coll A., 'Eilean I' in *Am Measg nam Bodach* (Glasgow, 1938), pp. 25–33.

MacFarlane's Geographical Collections, vol. II, Scottish History Society, vol. LII (Edinburgh, 1907).

Maclean, Lachlan, *An Historical Account of Iona from the Earliest Period*, 1st edn (Edinburgh, 1833).

MacMillan, Revd Archibald, *Iona: Its History and Antiquities* (London, Edinburgh and Glasgow, 1898). Carved stones illustrated by Robert Brydall, FSA Scotland.

MacPhail, J. R. N. (ed.), *Highland Papers Vol. I 1337–1680*, Scottish History Society, second ser., vol. V (Edinburgh, 1914).

MacPhail, J. R. N., 'The Cleansing of I-colum-cille' in *Scottish Historical Review*, vol. 22 (1925), pp. 14–24.

Macquarrie, Alan and MacArthur, E. Mairi, *Iona through the Ages*, 2nd edn (Coll, 1992).

Martin, Martin, *A Description of the Western Islands of Scotland*, 1st edn (London, 1703).

Maxwell, William, *Iona and the Ionians* (Glasgow, 1857).

Meek, Donald, 'Modern Celtic Christianity: the Contemporary "Revival" and its Roots' in *The Scottish Bulletin of Evangelical Theology*, vol. 10, no. 1 (spring 1992), pp. 6–31.

Meek, Donald (forthcoming), 'Modern Celtic Christianity', paper presented at workshop on Celts and Celticism held in the Royal Irish Academy, Dublin, May 1993, under the auspices of the European Science Foundation.

Millar, Jean, *Flowers of Iona*, new edn (Iona, 1993). First edn 1972.

Munro, R. W., *Monro's Western Isles of Scotland* (Edinburgh and London, 1961). Edition of Dean Monro's 'Description' of 1549 from a hitherto unpublished manuscript.

Pennant, Thomas, *A Tour in Scotland and Voyage to the Hebrides 1772*, 2 vols (London, 1776).

Pococke, Bishop R., *Pococke's Tours in Scotland*, ed. by D. W. Kemp, Scottish History Society, vol. I (Edinburgh, 1887).

Proceedings of the Society of Antiquaries of Scotland. Revd T. MacLaughlan, 'Notice of Monoliths in the Island of Mull' (1863), pp. 48–50; J. Drummond, 'Notice of One of the Supposed Burial Places of St Columba' (1873–4), pp. 613–19; W. F. Skene, 'Notes on the Early Establishments at Iona' (1874–5), pp. 330–49; A. O. Curle, 'Iona Nunnery Finds' (1923–4), pp. 102–11; M. Redknap, 'Abbey Excavations 1976' (1976–7), pp. 228–53; G. Ritchie and A. Lane, 'Dun Bhuirg' (1978–80), pp. 209–29; J. W. Barber, 'Excavations on Iona 1979' (1981), pp. 282–380.

Purser, John, *Scotland's Music* (Edinburgh, 1992).

Reeves, William, *Adamnani Vitae Sancti Columbae* (Dublin, 1857).

Richmond, James C., *A Visit to Iona by an American Clergyman* (Glasgow, 1849).

Ritchie, A. and Ritchie, E., *Iona Past and Present with Maps*, 3rd edn (Edinburgh, 1934). First published 1928.

Ross, Alexander J., *Memoir of Alexander Ewing D.C.L. Bishop of Argyll and the Isles* (London, 1877).

Ross, Anne, *The Folklore of the Scottish Highlands*, paperback edn (London, 1990). First edn 1976.

Sacheverell, William, *An Account of the Isle of Man ... with a voyage to I-Columb-Kill* (London, 1701).

Skene, W. F., *Celtic Scotland*, 3 vols (Edinburgh, 1876 (vol. 1), 1877 (vol. 2), 1880 (vol. 3)).

Smith, Revd John, *The Life of St Columba* (Edinburgh, 1798).

Smyth, Alfred P., *Warlords and Holy Men: Scotland AD 80–1000* (Edinburgh, 1989). First published 1984.

Stewart, John, *Wilson's Official Guide to the Islands of Staffa and Iona* (Glasgow and London, 1886).

Statistical Account of Scotland, 'Parish of Kilfinichen & Kilviceuen'. First: Revd Dugald Campbell, vol. XIV (Edinburgh, 1795); second: Revd Donald Campbell, vol. VII (Edinburgh, 1845); third: Revd Ewan MacLean, vol. IX (Edinburgh, 1958).

Viner, David, *The Iona Marble Quarry*, new edn (Iona, 1992). First edn 1979.

Walker, Revd Dr John, *Report on the Hebrides of 1764 and 1771*, ed. M. M. McKay (Edinburgh, 1980); id., *An Economical History of the Hebrides and Highlands of Scotland*, 2 vols (Edinburgh, 1808).

Walsh, J. R. and Bradley, T., *A History of the Irish Church 400–700 AD* (Dublin, 1991).

Note: an extensive list of published and manuscript accounts by travellers to Iona is included in the author's PhD thesis, *The Island of Iona: Aspects of its Social and Economic History from 1750 to 1914* (Edinburgh University, 1989).

Index